The
Garland Library
of
War and Peace

The
Garland Library
of
War and Peace

Under the General Editorship of

Blanche Wiesen Cook, *John Jay College,* C.U.N.Y.

Sandi E. Cooper, *Richmond College,* C.U.N.Y.

Charles Chatfield, *Wittenberg University*

Title No. *275*

Volume No. *239*

An American Peace Policy

by
Kirby Page

with an Introduction by
John H. Clarke
*Former Associate of the Supreme Court
of the United States*

and a new Introduction
for the Garland Edition by
Charles DeBenedetti

Garland Publishing, Inc., New York
1971

Introduction

In 1925, a succession of remarkable forces converged for the first time in the history of American peace politics. Within a few months, there took place a broad-based movement for accession to the World Court; the completion of a Harmony Plan of conciliation among the nation's peace leadership; and a mass campaign to mobilize college students behind the movement toward international peace. Overlapping and interacting, these three forces moved toward a resolution in December in the scheduled Senate debate over the World Court issue. Gathering momentum, they managed progressively to set the essential boundaries of peace activism across the country. And they determined, in practice, the intellectual framework in which Kirby Page built his case for An American Peace Policy.

With an easy mien and probing intelligence, Kirby Page had already established himself by 1925 as a leading exponent of liberal Christianity and religious pacifism. Born in 1890 in the East Texas town of Fred, Page was ordained a minister of the Disciples of Christ after graduating from Drake University in Des Moines, Iowa. In 1916, after one year of graduate work at the University of Chicago, he volunteered for service as a YMCA secretary with Allied troops in the

5

British Isles and along the Western Front. The carnage that he encountered there quickly confirmed him in his awakening pacifist faith. Frustrated by the anomoly of Christian service in inhuman war, the young minister resigned from YMCA service and accepted a staff position with G. Sherwood Eddy, an international secretary for the YMCA and a powerful voice of the Social Gospel. Page accompanied Eddy in visits to Europe and Asia until 1918, when he departed in order to become pastor at the Ridgewood Church of Christ in Brooklyn. He served there until July, 1921, when he re-joined Eddy as a full-time, free-lance associate. For the next four years, until he assumed the editorship of The World Tomorrow, *Page devoted himself to preaching and writing in a headlong effort to develop a Christian perspective on the immediate issues of social justice and world peace.*

Page's absorption in the possibilities of peace and social justice acquainted him on a first-hand basis with the many-angled division within peace movement politics. Since 1920 organized peace activity was locked in debate over the means by which the United States could most satisfactorily effect discipline in an international (i.e., European) order prone to catastrophic violence. At its simplest angle, the debate divided cooperationists, who favored collaboration with multilateral agencies like the League of Nations and the World Court, and unilateralists, who urged Americans to uphold the ideal of world peace by their independent example and by their voluntary defense of international law. But the division had other ramifications as well. In organizational terms, it ranged Eastern pro-League groups like the League of Nations Non-Partisan Association against Midwestern anti-League agencies like the American Committee for the Outlawry of War. In liberal politics, the division over the disposition of American power in Europe strained relations within the sizable progressive element of the movement. Some liberals like John Dewey and Raymond Robins resented the corrosive influence of Old World politics upon American democracy, while others like Paul U. Kellogg and Raymond Fosdick favored the extension of international democracy through closer American supervision of European affairs.

Predictably, the conflict among progressives spilled into the liberal wing of American Protestantism, where ministers defined the meaning of peace according to their attitude toward the American role in Europe. Pacifists, too, were split over the form of American participation in European affairs. While Page and Eddy urged their fellow pacifists to organize behind established agencies of international co-operation, the Reverend John Haynes Holmes and Oswald Garrison Villard disparaged the existing structure of world organization and argued for the unilateral pursuit of the American global mission. Finally, from the angle of national politics, the differences among anti-war forces took on impor-

tance insofar as they placed Idaho Senator William E. Borah, the most influential political figure within the movement, emphatically on the side of the minority dissidents who opposed the standing agencies of world order. Most peace leaders agreed upon one point. If the movement was ever to advance in united fashion, Borah would have to be reconciled to the majority position or his influence broken.

The importance of the relationship between Borah and organized peace activism increased in 1925, as battle lines formed over the Republican Administration's two-year old plan to attach the nation to the World Court. Support for the proposal was impressive. Nearly every public pressure group, from American Legionnaires through non-resistant pacifists, favored the Administration's plan for entrance into the Court upon the basis of four specific reservations. Yet an influential minority of national political and peace leaders resented association with "European" peace agencies and argued instead for American leadership in the outlawry of the legal institution of war. Behind Borah and other Irreconcilable leaders, anti-Court spokesmen massed formidable political resistance to the Court juggernaut and succeeded in keeping the issue in suspense throughout the year.

President Calvin Coolidge reacted to the rising opposition to the Court proposal with a characteristic display of calculation and caution. Sensitive to Borah's attempts to extend his influence among both the Old Guard and progressive wings of the G.O.P., Collidge treated the Idahoan with deference and scrupulously avoided any temptation to engage in an open confrontation. The President properly identified Borah as his most serious rival for national leadership. Yet he was clearly anxious to avoid alienating the Senator and other anti-Court Republicans and risking the disruption of Party unity. Inevitably, Coolidge's solicitous treatment of the Court opposition contributed to recurring rumors throughout the spring that the President was about to strike a compromise with Borah at the Court's expense. Despite the consensus in their favor, pro-Court peace leaders rightly suspected the sincerity of Coolidge's commitment to the success of the Court plan and feared Borah's influence.

Disturbed by the wavering in Washington, Page, Eddy, and a small group of Protestant peace spokesmen called upon a number of national peace leaders to meet in a harmony session in June at the Hotel McAlpin in New York. It was their intention to develop a plan of conciliation that would unite the movement behind both the World Court and the Outlawry of War idea and, in the process, provide an advanced common ground for the international positions of Coolidge and Borah. Meeting in the worst heat of the New York summer, a representative collection of anti-war activists concluded a compromise agreement after three days of difficult debate. It was a tense, trying experience that

INTRODUCTION

Columbia University Professor James T. Shotwell later recalled as "the hardest job I have ever undertaken." Bodies sweated. Nerves frayed. And several times the men "were on the point of losing our tempers, or rather lost our tempers and didn't say so, and then at last we managed to sign up." [1] *Especially, the final agreement provided for American accession to the World Court upon the condition that, if Court members failed within a five year period to outlaw international war, the United States was obliged to withdraw. The conferees delayed publication of the compromise for three weeks, while they contacted other potential signatories. Then, on July 15, they released the accord to the press and officially initiated their unity campaign. Within two months, its more ardent supporters began referring to the agreement as "The New Harmony Peace Program for America."*

The Harmony Plan gave new direction to the work of Kirby Page. Inspired by the unexpected success of peace unity, the young minister turned to assist the World Court Committee of the Council of Christian Associations, the agency of the Student Christian Movement of America, in laying plans for an extensive campaign upon the nation's campuses. At the suggestion of Henry Van Dusen, executive secretary of the World Court Committee, Page produced An

[1] *James T. Shotwell to Tasker H. Bliss, June 29, 1925, Box 269, Tasker Howard Bliss Papers, Manuscript Division, Library of Congress. James T. Shotwell, The Autobiography of James T. Shotwell (Indianapolis, 1961), p. 195.*

10

INTRODUCTION

American Peace Policy *as a handbook for the student
movement. And, over the next six months, Van
Dusen and the Committee directed the distribution of
25,000 copies on campuses across the country. Page
himself travelled over 40,000 miles during the last
half of the year in order to speak at 46 different
colleges and at 13 state and regional conferences in
behalf of the Harmony agreement and the larger
American Peace Policy. He defended the coalition
agreement with two arguments. It was first of all a
valuable political alternative in the event that stale-
mate in Washington between the Administration and
Borah led to a search for compromise. In the second
place, it served as an educational device which
demonstrated that the Court was merely the first of
many steps that America must take toward the
abolition of all war.*

*As Page preached, the World Court Committee
worked assiduously to mobilize student opinion
behind the Court resolution. The organization
despatched speakers, sponsored conferences, and dis-
tributed literature. It completed a massive public
opinion poll that registered the votes of over 130,000
students at 333 colleges and universities. And it even
plotted the possibility of a mass student march upon
a recalcitrant Congress. In the end, the Committee
hailed the outpouring of student support for the
Court as the largest expression of organized university
sentiment in the country's history. Page and other
American peace leaders felt confident that they had*

11

helped to introduce an active new participant into national politics.[2]

Unfortunately for Page, student peace activism declined soon after the Senate began debate in December on the Court bill. The Harmony Plan did no better. The agreement tottered briefly and then collapsed utterly in December, as the Court issue headed toward a Senate vote and peace partisans divided once again along former lines. While the Plan slipped into oblivion, peace leaders fell into new debate over the reasons for the failure of unity. The ensuing argument left only two matters clear. The agreement never attracted the support of either Coolidge or Borah. And its collapse intensified friction within the movement. The one achievement that survived the Harmony effort was An American Peace Policy.

An American Peace Policy *was an excellent expression of the peace plans of the pacifist-institutionalist left in post-war America. With eminent clarity, Page argued for the institutionalization of pacific alternatives to war and pleaded for the elimination of instruments of force from the building structure of world order. In his vision, modern commerce and industry had created patterns of rich but volatile international interdependence. Operating in delicate intricacy, the modern state system stood*

[2] *See "Student Opinion and the World Court: The Report of the National Director to the World Court Committee of the Council of Christian Associations," January 2, 1926, in folder: Henry P. Van Dusen, Box 87, Salmon O. Levinson Papers, University of Chicago.*

helpless before the disequilibrium generated by nationalism and scientific weaponry and in desperate need of rational organization and total disarmament. The fundamental needs of international politics, Page concluded, were about to blend out of sheer necessity with the ideals of pacific Christianity. The pacifist ethic and non-violent modes of diplomatic settlement were finally becoming the politically necessary—and not only the humanly responsible—means of accommodating inexorable international pressure toward world interdependence.

In addition to its persuasive political argument, An American Peace Policy *was informed by an arresting expression of faith and hope. Like an ancient prophet, the fervent Disciples of Christ minister hearkened to the ominous signs of human frailty and failure even as he inspired readers with hope for the world that "faith and works" will bring.*[3] *Page had precious little evidence that contemporary political leaders were prepared to act upon the bond that he saw developing between pacifist ethics and international political necessity. Nor had he any reason to believe that his generation was seriously committed to "pay the price of peace and justice."*[4] *Yet he was a man who could not help but hope. Radically optimistic about the possibilities of mankind, Page was determined to prod his generation to action by a succession of spiritual summons. His challenge was*

[3] *See below, p. 84.*
[4] *See below, p. 10.*

13

not, of course, taken up. But neither has it been dulled. Rather the challenge and appeal of his thoughts remain tenaciously with us. And the question of whether or not our generation is prepared to pay the price of peace—or at least make a substantial down payment toward its realization—is one that stands essentially in the same terms that he described a half-century ago.

Charles De Benedetti
Department of History
University of Toledo

AN AMERICAN PEACE POLICY

KIRBY PAGE

AN AMERICAN
PEACE POLICY

BY

KIRBY PAGE

Author of "War: Its Causes, Consequences and Cure,"
"Imperialism aud Nationalism," "The Sword or the
Cross," Co-author of "The Abolition of War."

WITH AN INTRODUCTION ¡BY

JOHN H. CLARKE

FORMER ASSOCIATE JUSTICE OF THE SUPREME CORT
OF THE UNITED STATES

NEW YORK
GEORGE H. DORAN COMPANY

AN AMERICAN PEACE POLICY
— c —
PRINTED IN THE UNITED STATES OF AMERICA

INTRODUCTION

In this little book, Mr. Page presents in an original, illuminating, and authoritative manner, and in much smaller compass than they may be found elsewhere, the facts and reasons which make it convincingly clear: that steam and electricity and commerce have so bound the nations together in this modern world that for our government, as for every other, the isolation of unrestrained nationalism is impossible; that the only rational prospect of preventing the coming of desolating wars is through some form of self imposed, permanent, international organization; and that the World Court, the Outlawry of War, and ultimately the League of Nations, perhaps somewhat modified in scope and character, are the most promising agencies for such organization which have as yet been devised.

It is abundantly shown herein that the United States is bound by every consideration of national interest and of national honor to participate in the World Court and to aid in its development and support. This should no longer be considered an open question, for it is denied only by a handful of perverse Senators who are thinking more of saving their faces than of serving their country.

The most novel, and it may prove to be the most important, part of Mr. Page's book is the chapter dealing with the Outlawry of War through the World Court. He here gives to the public the first authoritative statement of the program for the Outlawing of the War System by making resort to war as a process for settling international disputes an international crime, and by convincing illustration and argument he sustains the wisdom and practicability of such a plan. This program is very simple—many final solutions of great problems are

3

simple—and there are many advocates of peace who believe that in it may be found a new method of approach to international coöperation which will appeal to the millions of American citizens whose minds are closed against all approach to the League of Nations, which the campaign of 1920 led them to fear as "an evil thing with a holy name," which would be much more likely to involve us in international wars, than to preserve us from them.

The process of world organization thus proposed is this: (1) Immediate entry into the World Court with the Harding-Coolidge reservations, but with a declaration of purpose on the part of our government to invite all the nations to join us in making resort to war a crime under international law; (2) an international conference shall be called to frame a Code of international law, with the Outlawry of War as its fundamental principle, which shall be much more comprehensive—shall deal with many more international relations—than is the existing body of international law; and (3) when such a Code is adopted by the nations the World Court shall be given obligatory jurisdiction over all disputes falling within the scope of its provisions. The United States shall also declare that it will withdraw from the Court if such a code as is proposed shall not be adopted within five years.

There are those of us who agree with Mr. Page in thinking that a World Court even with such jurisdiction, under such a code, as is thus proposed, would not be adequate to dispose satisfactorily of all political, as distinguished from justiciable, disputes, and that a League of Nations in some form with processes of discussion, conciliation and arbitration would still be necessary to preserve the peace of the world. However, it is very clear that even a partial realization of this program would carry the nations much farther toward world peace than they are at present, or than they will be carried simply by our adhering to the World Court as it now is, and because it is so full of promising advance toward larger international coöperation in some form, many of the friends of peace are uniting to give the proposal their wholehearted support, to the end that its merits may have a full discussion and a fair trial.

This Outlawry of War conception is of distinctly American origin and "We must Outlaw War" is an inspiring slogan which appeals to the minds and hearts of us all as no other form of peace proposal can, by associating war with the murder that it is and by condemning it as a crime against both religion and civilization.

Substantially all of the men and women of our country, and of every other, are deeply opposed to the war system, and the only reason why they have not united long since to banish it from the world is that the advocates of peace have not been able to agree among themselves as to the form of an agency to supplant it. This simple Outlawry program, which may appropriately be called "The New Harmony Peace Program for America," is the result of concession as to the method for achieving the great end, made in a spirit, which, if it were to become general, would result, I am sure, in an invincible union of the friends of peace. It must be added that there is something of this disposition to sink unessentials in my approval of this little book, for Mr. Page is much more of a pacifist than I am, especially in his hostility to resort to force as an ultimate sanction for decisions of the Court or League, but we are both determined to go forward together as far as is possible, in our efforts, humble though they be, to substitute reason and law, discussion and arbitration, which are civilization's ways of settling international disputes, for irrational, brutal war which is the savage way.

JOHN H. CLARKE

CONTENTS

AN AMERICAN PEACE POLICY

CHAPTER I

RESULTS OF ECONOMIC INTERDEPEND-ENCE AND POLITICAL DIVISION

"The world is going well. The Prince of Peace is coming to His own. Let us eat and drink and give our gifts with thankfulness this year, and patient hope." Thus ran the concluding words of an editorial on "The Progress of Peace" in Harper's Weekly, December 11, 1909; the editor at that time being George Harvey, later Ambassador to Great Britain. In November, 1911, President Taft published an important article under the title: "The Dawn of World Peace." An editorial in the Dial, on April 1, 1914, only four months before the beginning of the World War, said: "The civilized world is slowly groping its way toward organic unity and purpose; rivalry is giving way to coöperative action; and the motives that precipitate nations headlong into conflict are visibly becoming weaker."

These utterances are merely a reflection of the spirit of optimism concerning the prospects for peace which prevailed in many quarters during the period immediately preceding the outbreak of the war. True enough, voices of warning were being raised, but the rank and file of people, both in the United States and on the continent of Europe, were utterly oblivious to the signs of the time. The war came as an almost total surprise to the masses of people everywhere. The historian of the present day in surveying the trend of events during the first fourteen years of this century is astounded at the blindness and carelessness of the populace and the stupidity and impotence of the leaders in the face of the approaching catastrophe. Only an infinitesimal fraction of people or

9

leaders anywhere desired war. The war came because
they continued to maintain attitudes and to engage in
practices which made conflict inevitable. They were
unwilling to pay the price of peace.

There are many parallels between the present international situation and that which prevailed during the
decade prior to the war. There is still a colossal amount
of popular ignorance concerning international relations,
as well as much criminal negligence on the part of leaders.
The same attitudes and practices which led to the World
War are still doing their deadly work and if continued will
surely lead to another great conflict. Peoples and leaders
alike are still unwilling to pay the price of peace and
justice. In order to understand more fully just what that
price is, let us examine certain basic facts of modern
international relationships.

MODERN INDUSTRIALISM

Science and industrialism are binding the peoples of
the earth together with cords of iron and steel and gold.
Inventions in the realm of communication and transportation have made the world into a neighborhood. It is
infinitely easier to send a message around the world now
than across a county a century ago. Merchandise is now
transported from continent to continent with more ease
than from state to state a hundred years ago. This
advance in communication and transportation has made
possible the intensification and expansion of modern
industrialism. Nations everywhere are becoming more
and more industrialized. This fact has an exceedingly
important bearing upon international relations. The
more highly industrialized a nation becomes the more
dependent it is upon the other parts of the world. Industrial nations must secure huge quantities of raw materials
—coal, iron, oil, rubber, timber, food, etc.—from other
lands. They engage in mass production and therefore

produce more goods than can profitably be sold within their own borders. Consequently they must have access to customers in other countries. Moreover, they tend to accumulate more capital than can profitably be invested at home, so foreign fields of investment are needed. Industrialism has vastly increased production and has thereby made possible a huge increase in population. Herbert Hoover has called attention to the fact that Europe now has an excess population of 100 million people who can be kept alive only by the efficient and continuous operation of world-wide industrial organization. Thus we see that the peoples of the earth are being inextricably linked together.

ENTANGLEMENTS OF THE UNITED STATES

The United States is becoming more and more industrialized and is therefore increasingly involved in international affairs. Foreign trade is assuming an ever larger place in the life of the nation. The value of American imports rose from 1,813 million dollars in 1913 to 3,450 millions in 1924, while the value of exports rose from 2,466 millions in 1913 to 4,311 millions in 1924.[1] In the matter of raw materials the United States is far more self-sufficient than any other great nation, and yet in several important respects we are dependent upon imports. This is notably true of crude rubber and crude oil. "The world's export of rubber in the year 1923 was valued at $240,000,000 of which the United States imported $185,000,000 worth, or 77 percent of the total. Ninety-five percent of the rubber used today comes from plantations located in one geographical region—southeastern Asia and the neighboring islands—and in districts under the control of Great Britain, Holland and France."[2] The United States produces about 60 percent of the

[1] The New York Nation, May 27, 1925, p. 599.
[2] Harry N. Whitford, Foreign Affairs, June 15, 1924, p. 613.

world's supply of oil, and yet we are a heavy importer of oil. Concerning future prospects Sir John Cadman, former Chairman of the Inter-Allied Petroleum Council, said: "Before 1930 the United States may easily be relying upon foreign sources of supply for at least half, possibly more than half, of the oil demanded by her domestic requirements."[1] Mr. Herbert Hoover has sounded a note of warning in these words: "Unless our nationals reënforce and increase their holdings abroad, we shall be dependent upon other nations for the supply of this vital commodity within a measurable number of years. The truth of the matter is that other countries have conserved their oil at the expense of our own. We must go into foreign fields and in a big way."[2]

Not only in the matter of imports but also with regard to exports, the United States is bound up with the rest of the world. Of the world's total supply of basic necessities, Judge Gary has estimated that the United States, with only 6 percent of the world's population and 7 percent of the world's land, produces the following proportions:[3] iron and steel 40 percent, lead 40 percent, silver 40 percent, zinc 50 percent, coal 52 percent, aluminum 60 percent, copper 60 percent, wheat 25 percent, corn 75 percent. The future prosperity of this country, as well as the welfare of the peoples of other lands, is dependent upon heavy exports of our surplus goods.[4]

Enormous sums of American capital are now being invested in foreign fields. Whereas the total amount of American foreign investments in 1913 was between one and two billion dollars, this amount had risen above nine billions at the beginning of 1925, divided as follows:[5]

---

[1]Quoted in Our World, August, 1923, p. 27.
[2]Quoted in The New Republic, August 20, 1924.
[3]Address on May 28, 1920.
[4]See an important article by C. K. Leith, The Political Control of Mineral Resources, Foreign Affairs, July 1925, pp. 541-555.
[5]See significant article by Herbert Feis, The Export of American Capital, Foreign Affairs, July 1925, pp. 667-686.

VALUE OF AMERICAN INVESTMENTS ABROAD
(Estimated, in millions of dollars, at the end of 1924)

Region	Gov't and Gov't Guaranteed Obligations	All other Investments	Total
Canada and Newfoundland......	1060	1400	2460
Latin America........	840	3200	4040
Europe..............	1500	400	1900
Asia and Oceania......	440	250	690
	3840	5250	9090

During the single year of 1924 citizens of the United States invested $1,268,438,394[1] in foreign securities. And during the first six months of 1925 another half billion dollars was added to the total overseas investments of American citizens. The net interest income of the United States from abroad reached 464 millions in 1924; this being the net amount after deductions had been made for interest on the three billions of foreign investments in the United States. The overseas investments of our citizens are likely to increase steadily, especially so since we now possess approximately half of the entire gold supply of the world.

Moreover, the nations of Europe are indebted to the United States for war loans to an extent of eleven billion dollars, as follows:

UNITED STATES WAR LOANS

Great Britain..................	$4,661,000,000
France.....................	3,847,521,000
Italy.........................	2,015,079,000
Russia.........................	236,726,000
Belgium.......................	190,013,000
Greece.......................	16,500,000
Roumania.....................	15,507,000
	$10,982,346,000

[1]Current History Magazine, March 1925, Section on World Finance.

In addition to these amounts $878,664,000 was advanced by the United States to the various countries for relief and reconstruction, making a grand total of $11,861,010,-000.[1]

With a total of 21 billion dollars in overseas loans and investments—an amount larger than the entire national wealth of Canada and twice the total wealth of Belgium— the United States is bound with cords of gold to practically every other country in the world. Hundreds of thousands, perhaps millions, of American citizens are holders of foreign securities, and consequently are financially concerned with international relations. The whole tendency of modern commerce and finance is to make the entire world an economic unity. In such a world isolation— splendid or otherwise—becomes an utter impossibility.

NATIONALISM

In contrast with the economic interdependence of the peoples of the earth is their political division. Mankind is divided into about sixty nations, each of which claims absolute sovereignty. Nationalism is one of the mightiest forces with which we must reckon. And yet it is in large part an artificial creation. It does not spring from any one source. The factors which combine to produce nationalism are: race, language, geography, religion, culture, history and tradition, common economic interests. Nationalism is a sentiment. Professor Zimmerman says: "Nationality, like religion, is subjective; psychological; a condition of mind; a spiritual possession; a way of feeling, thinking and living." Patriotism is one of the most powerful of all sentiments, and coupled with the theory of national sovereignty, is one of the major divisive forces of our day. National boundaries tend to become international barriers. The peoples of the various nations are taught that they are different from, and of course

[1]Harvey E. Fisk, The Inter-Ally Debts, p. 349.

superior to, other peoples. Each nation exaggerates its own virtues and underestimates its own faults, while depreciating the good qualities of other nations and grossly distorting their vices. This combination leads to fear, suspicion and hatred. Thus is generated a temper which endangers friendly relations between nations. Within recent months Mr. Austin Chamberlain, Secretary of Foreign Affairs of Great Britain, has said: "Fear— haunting, restless, brooding fear—haunts the councils of every nation and the home of every continental people. Fear which renews day by day the offences of the war, the bitterness of the war, the rancours of the war. If this continues, sooner or later, Europe will march to a new Armageddon."

The situation would be less menacing if it were possible for nations to live by themselves, with only a minimum of contacts with other peoples. But modern industrialism has forever destroyed the possibility of any civilized nation living aloof from the rest of the world. A major consequence, therefore, of economic interdependence and political division is *imperialism*. If an industrial nation is to achieve and maintain power, wealth and prestige, it must have access to raw materials, markets and fields of investment outside its own borders. In a world of nationalism, with its consequent division, fear, suspicion and enmity, and a world of industrialism, with its interdependence, imperialism is an almost inevitable consequence. National interest demands uninterrupted access to backward parts of the earth with rich stores of raw materials and millions of potential customers. Therefore political and economic control of these areas becomes a dominant desire of industrial nations.

In seeking to be successful in this imperialistic struggle, the various nations maintain heavy armaments. Thus imperialism leads to *militarism*. In order to protect national honor and national interests the peoples of

Europe spent 40 billion dollars upon armies and navies during the period from 1871 to 1913, the rank in total expenditures for armaments being: France 8568 million dollars, Great Britain 8401 millions, Russia 7581 millions, Germany 7434 millions.[1] But even with huge armies and navies, nations do not feel secure, so they form *military alliances*. Alliances lead to counter-alliances, culminating in the *balance of power* system, with continents divided into two great armed camps. In such a world any overt act that threatens to disturb the balance of power, even though in itself it may possess only minor significance, instantly becomes a potential cause of war. During the decades prior to the war, crisis after crisis brought Europe to the verge of war. Finally the murder of an arch-duke, by threatening to disrupt the empire of Austria-Hungary and thus leave Germany without a strong ally, precipitated the World War.

So long as the spirit of unqualified national sovereignty prevails in a world that is economically interdependent, that long will imperialism, militarism, military alliances, the balance of power, crises and war hover as an ever-present menace over the peoples of the earth. "To the fierceness of private trade competition," says Mr. Wm. S. Culbertson, of the United States Tariff Commission, "has been added national competition; and trade rivalry, instead of being checked, has been intensified and stamped with a national stamp. It may be predicted that this nationalist competitive system, if allowed to continue the course pursued by it in recent decades, will, like Samson in the temple of the Philistines, destroy itself."[2] One does not need to be an alarmist to sound a warning concerning the probable effects of another great war. Not only are military and naval weapons becoming

---

[1]Harvey E. Fisk, French Public Finance, p. 1.

[2]International Economic Policies, p. 20. This is a very comprehensive and valuable discussion of the economic aspect of international problems.

vastly more destructive, but the increasing interdependence of mankind makes more and more calamitous the economic and financial disruption caused by war. So imminent and grave is the peril that even such a cautious spokesman as Herbert Hoover, in an Armistice Day address in Los Angeles, said: "The world has learned many lessons from the war, but none more emphatic than that its increasing terribleness will, if repeated again, destroy civilization itself. The mobilization of a whole people into war, the inventions of science turned to destruction and the killing of men will make any other great war the *cemetery of civilization.*"

CHAPTER II

WHAT KIND OF INTERNATIONAL ORGANIZATION IS NEEDED?

An American humorist recently said that the best way to deal with two nations which cannot get along together is to "move 'em away from each other." Unfortunately modern invention has made this forever impossible. We have by no means reached the closing chapter in the story of inventions in the realm of communication and transportation. Industrialism is in its early stages in many parts of the world. India, Japan and China are rapidly being industrialized. It is therefore a matter of life and death for civilization that some way be found to break the vicious circle—nationalism, imperialism, militarism, alliances, balance of power, crises, war—in which the peoples of the earth have been travelling. Since the nations cannot be kept apart, it is absolutely imperative that non-violent means of settling their disputes be devised. This means that international organization must be created. Wars will continue until adequate international machinery is available for the amicable adjustment of disputes between nations. If peace is to be preserved the nations must agree, in advance of a controversy, concerning the manner of its settlement. That is to say, law must be created.

LEGISLATION, ADMINISTRATION, ADJUDICATION

There are three stages in the process of substituting reasoned agreement or law for violence: some effective means of reaching an agreement, some way of administering the agreement, and some agency to interpret its meaning; that is, legislation, administration, adjudication; although it should be pointed out that this chronological order has not always been followed. The whole history of mankind demonstrates conclusively that legislative

18

bodies, executive officers and courts have been necessary to the preservation of peace between individuals, between groups and between states. Is it not obvious that all three are likewise essential to the preservation of peace between nations? A vast network of international agreements are now in operation. Many of these were the result of direct negotiation between two nations and are in the form of special treaties; many others were the outgrowth of international conferences of one kind or another and are embodied in general treaties. Codification of existing international law is a next step in the substitution of agreement for violence in international relations. Of the thousands of international agreements now in force, many are confused and lacking in clarity, and others are contradictory. It is obvious, however, that codification would not be a complete solution of the problem, because there are vast realms in international relations where existing agreements are wholly inadequate. The creation of new international law is imperatively demanded. As the number and variety of contacts between nations increase, the need for *permanent agencies* through which international agreements may be reached becomes more obvious and more pressing. The hope of peace lies in the increased willingness of nations to enter into and abide by international agreements.

The history of civilization is a record of the expansion of the sphere of law and orderly processes of government. As human contacts have widened it has been necessary to extend the jurisdiction of government, from family to tribe, from city to feudal-state, from state to nation. Government, if it is to be effective, must be based upon reality. Its scope must be as wide as the extent of the vital problems with which it must deal. National governments are utterly unable to solve many of the complex and dangerous problems of the modern world. Nothing less than international agencies will suffice. Finance, commerce, transportation, communication, armaments, health, morality—all these have phases which are essentially international in scope. The problems here involved cannot be solved within national boundaries. National government is without adequate jurisdiction to curb evils which are world-wide in extent. It is only by international agreements that such problems can effectively be dealt with. Such international agreements, the beginnings of international legislation, are absolutely essential to the preservation of civilization.

We are not suggesting that international agencies be empowered to legislate in all departments of life for the whole world. The jurisdiction of any international agency of justice should be clearly defined and should be restricted to problems which are undeniably international in character and which cannot be solved by national action. The precedent set by the thirteen states in creating the Federal Government of the United States is of great value at this point. All powers not specifically delegated to the Union were reserved by the states. Certainly at the beginning, only a minimum number of problems should be brought within the jurisdiction of international agencies.

The effectiveness of an agreement depends in large measure upon the way in which it is carried out. Many of the international agreements now being reached are very complex in their nature and require the continuous attention of trained executives to insure their successful operation. The need for an extensive international civil service, composed of the highest type of statesmen and the most skilled technical experts from the various countries, is unquestioned by all careful students of world problems.

The need for an international court is likewise undeniable. Disputes are constantly arising between nations which may lead to violence if not submitted to judicial settlement. In order to be effective a court must have

(1) an adequate basis of law upon which to base its decisions; (2) permanent judges of high ability, wide experience, and unquestioned moral integrity; (3) compulsory jurisdiction; (4) the confidence of the litigant nations. Thus we see that international agencies of legislation, administration and adjudication are required if peace is to be maintained. But even these three phases of international machinery are not adequate to meet all the threatening situations which may arise. Legislation, administration and adjudication all deal with law. But in this complex world there are many relationships not covered by law; emergencies are constantly arising which had not been foreseen by lawmakers. Therefore, *permanent agencies of mediation, conciliation and arbitration* are required if crises are to be dealt with effectively and amicably.

OUTLAWRY OF WAR[1]

International organization in itself is not sufficient to guarantee peace and justice. So long as the war system remains a legal method of settling disputes between nations that long will peace remain an elusive dream. Before permanent peace can be assured it is therefore necessary that a general treaty should be negotiated declaring war to be a crime under the law of nations. The exact means by which this international agreement shall be reached is relatively unimportant. The essential thing is that all legal countenance should be withdrawn from war by a general treaty, and that the peoples of the various nations should agree in advance not to resort to it and to restrain and punish their own war-makers.

Humanity must carry one stage further the process of

---

[1]The idea and phrase "outlawry of war" were first proposed by Mr. S. O. Levinson, an attorney of Chicago. For literature concerning outlawry, write to the American Committee for the Outlawry of War, 134 South La Salle St., Chicago.

outlawry. For long ages individual quarrels were settled by violence or by the duel. There came a time, however, when the settlement of individual disputes by armed combat was declared illegal and criminal. Murder and duelling did not thereupon disappear absolutely. They were, however, reduced to a minimum. Likewise, armed combat between groups, cities and states has been declared illegal and criminal. Civil war now occurs only at rare intervals, whereas formerly it occurred with great frequence. The action of the thirteen states of America in outlawing war between themselves is very illuminating. In Article 1, Section 10 of the Constitution of the United States, the thirteen states agreed to the following provision: "No State shall, without the Consent of Congress . . . keep troops or ships of war in time of peace, . . . or engage in war, unless actually invaded, or in such imminent danger as will not admit delay." They specifically agreed not to go to war with each other, but retained the right of self defense if attacked.

It should be emphasized that disarmament has always been essential to the effective functioning of agencies of justice. If it were customary for all citizens to go armed, the effectiveness of courts would be greatly impaired. If cities still retained armed forces to be used against other cities, state governments would be impotent to preserve the peace. If our various states had each retained a standing army and navy to protect itself against the other states, our Federal Government would have been unable to prevent the frequent outbreak of hostilities. To make really effective the outlawry of war, the nations must agree ultimately to disarm all forces maintained for action against other nations. It should be pointed out that disarmament has rarely, if ever, been absolute. An individual may still secure a permit to go armed under special circumstances; cities still maintain their police force and states their militia. The important thing to note in this connection, however, is that *city police are never used to settle a dispute with another city; nor are state militia used against another state.* This is the goal toward which the nations must strive. Let each nation maintain a small police force sufficient to deal with its own criminal individuals and lawless groups, such as rioters, smugglers and pirates, and disarm all forces maintained for action against other nations.

SANCTIONS

How shall international agencies secure observance of agreements reached? How shall an international court enforce its decisions? It is frequently assumed that an international police force will be required. Lyman Abbot once pictured it this way: "The time is coming when all the military forces of the civilized world will be one police force, under one chief of police, with one international legislature to decide what is the will of the nations, with one international court to interpret the official and legal intelligence of the nations, and just enough navy to make the world safe, under a common direction and common control—and no more."[1] This is an extreme statement of a point of view which is widely held. Let us examine carefully its validity and practicability. Is it possible to create such an international police? Would it be an effective means of accomplishing the desired end? Is such a force necessary?

Concerning the possibility of abolishing all national armies and navies and maintaining only an international police force, does anyone who has had actual experience with the realities of the existing situation in Europe, and who is aware of the intensity of nationalism and patriotism, and the extent of fear and hatred, believe there is even the remotest possibility of accomplishing this momentous change in our generation? Even the most sanguine and

[1]The Outlook, June 30, 1906, p. 510.

optimistic of statesmen do not regard such a proposal as within the realm of practical politics. The most that seems possible is that the nations should be willing to place their own armed forces at the disposal of international agencies under certain conditions. What would happen if an international agency should attempt to use such a force against a nation? If the other nations were united against the guilty country, then the effort might prove successful. But suppose the nations were divided in sympathy, as is almost certain to be the case in any serious dispute, would not the effort to use armed force be likely to precipitate a general war? It has often been pointed out that when there is general agreement among the nations the use of armed force against a recalcitrant power is least needed, whereas when the nations are divided in sympathy, it is least effective.[1] In the light of these indisputable facts, is it not highly dangerous to use armed force in the effort to compel acceptance of decisions of an international body? Concerning this question, Mr. William Hard says: "The way of sanctions, I think, is the way to stultification by not enforcing them or the way to a cataclysm by trying to enforce them."[2] If it is quite out of the question to secure a genuinely international police under present conditions and if the proposal to authorize international agencies to make use of national armies and navies is too dangerous to justify its adoption, upon what measures shall international agencies rely for the enforcement of their decisions?

---

[1]Professor Quincy Wright of the University of Chicago, says: "Physical force is more difficult to apply to states than to individuals because: (1) the units are proportionately larger, (2) national sentiment prevents the creation of a unified police force, (3) punishment of a guilty nation by fines, indemnities or losses of terriotry is likely to undermine the economic structure of society and seriously to injure other nations, and (4) moral responsibility can not generally be attributed to one nation alone and never to the entire population of a nation, all of whom suffer." (American Journal of International Law, Vol. 19, p. 98).

[2]Annals of the American Academy, July 1925, p. 141.

SANCTIONS OF THE SUPREME COURT OF THE UNITED STATES[1]

Does not the procedure of the United States Supreme Court shed light upon this problem? Does the Supreme Court use armed force in compelling acceptance of *its decisions against states?* It does not, and never has. In its entire history of 138 years the Supreme Court has never used force against any state. As a matter of fact, the Constitution does not authorize the Supreme Court or the President of the United States to use armed force against a state which refuses to abide by a judicial decision. Section 2 of Article 3 of the Constitution defines the powers of the Supreme Court—"The judicial power shall extend to . . . controversies between two or more States"—but it is absolutely silent concerning means of enforcing the Court's decisions.

The reason for this silence is revealed in the record of the debates in the Constitutional Convention. The original draft of the Virginia Plan, written by James Madison and submitted to the Constitutional Convention, contained a provision authorizing the National Legislature "to call forth the force of the Union against any member of the Union failing to fulfill its duty under the articles thereof." This proposal provoked so much hostility that it was withdrawn within two days. Madison subsequently changed his mind with regard to this point and wrote: "The more he reflected on the use of force, the more he doubted the practicability, the justice and the efficacy of it when applied to people collectively, and not individually. A union of the States containing such an ingredient seemed to provide for its own destruction. The use of force against a State, would seem more like a declaration of war, than an infliction of punishment, and would probably be considered by the party attacked as a dissolution of all previous compacts by which it might

---
[1]See an important article by James N. Rosenberg, Brutum Fulmen: A Precedent for a World Court, Columbia Law Review, June, 1925, pp. 783-799.

be bound. He hoped that such a system would be found as might render this clause unnecessary, and moved that the clause be postponed."[1] On July 14, 1787, in discussing the proposed government, Mr. Madison "called for a single instance in which the General Government was not to operate on the people individually," and continued, without an answer having been interposed to his question, "the practicability of making laws, with coercive sanctions, for the States as political bodies has been exploded on all hands."[2]

Alexander Hamilton said: "A project of this kind (military coercion of States) is little less romantic than the monster-taming spirit, attributed to the fabulous heroes and demi-gods of antiquity."[3] Oliver Ellsworth, later Chief Justice of the Supreme Court, pointed out that "if we should attempt to execute the laws of the Union by sending an armed force against a delinquent state, it would involve the good and bad, the innocent and guilty, in the same calamity."[4] Mr. Ellsworth also said: "This Constitution does not attempt to coerce sovereign bodies, states, in their political capacity."[5] "As a matter of history," says Mr. Herbert A. Smith, "it is quite clear that most of the States would never have entered the Union if they had imagined that thereby they were submitting themselves to the possibility of Federal coercion."[6]

Concerning this question, James Brown Scott, of the Carnegie Endowment for International Peace, says: "It was foreseen that force might be necessary to execute the laws of the Union, and therefore Congress was specifically empowered by a clause of the eighth section

---

[1]James Madison's Notes of Debates in the Federal Convention of 1787, edited by James Brown Scott, p. 52.

[2]See James Brown Scott, The United States of America: A Study in International Organization, pp. 206-207.

[3]Ibid, p. 205.

[4]Ibid, p. 206.

[5]Jonathan Elliott, Debates on the Adoption of the Federal Constitution, Vol. 2, p. 197.

[6]The American Supreme Court as an International Tribunal, p. 101.

of the first article 'to provide for calling forth the militia to execute the laws of the Union, suppress insurrections and repel invasions.' But force is to be used, in accordance with the views previously set forth, against individuals whether they act singly or in small groups, as a mob or in organized masses as insurgents. The individual, not the State, suffers; the individual, not the State, is coerced. At least this seems to have been the view of the framers of the Constitution, and it has been the practice of the government of the more perfect Union of the North American States."[1]

In the Cherokee Nation case, Chief Justice Marshall said: "The bill requires us to control the legislature of Georgia, and to restrain the exertion of its physical force. The propriety of such an interposition by the court may be well questioned."[2] In the Denison case in 1860, Chief Justice Taney said: "But if the Governor of Ohio refuses to discharge this duty, there is no power delegated to the general government, either through the Judicial Department or any other department, to use any coercive means to compel him."[3]

It should be pointed out, however, that recently the tendency has been for the Supreme Court judges to assume that they have power to enforce decisions against states. This view was expressed by Chief Justice White in the Virginia case, and yet even in this case no force was applied. Throughout the 138 years of its existence, the Supreme Court has consistently refrained from using armed troops or policemen in enforcing its decisions against states. It is worth pointing out that even in the case of the Civil War, the Government at Washington maintained that it was not waging war against the Southern States but was seeking to put down a rebellion of its own citizens.

[1]J. B. Scott, The United States of America, pp. 206, 207.
[2]Cherokee Nation v. Georgia, (U. S. 1831) 5 Pet. 1, 20.
[3]Kentucky v. Denison (U. S. 1860) 24 Howard 66, 109-110.

If then, the Supreme Court has not attempted to use force in coercing a state, upon what has it relied to secure acceptance of its decisions? Two things: (1) the agreement of the people of the various states to abide by such decisions; (2) the power of public opinion. In general the decisions of the Supreme Court have been accepted faithfully by the states. The record, however, is not perfect. In fact, the first decree against a state was disobeyed. In the Chisholm case in 1792 the Court held that it had the right to entertain a suit by a private individual against the State of Georgia. Thereupon the legislature of that state declared the decision unconstitutional and passed a law providing that any person attempting to enforce the court's decision should be "guilty of felony" and should "suffer death by being hanged."[1] The other twelve states sided with Georgia against the Court, with the result that the Eleventh Amendment was passed. Wisconsin challenged the Supreme Court's decision in the Booth case.[2] In 1915 a judgment was awarded against West Virginia in favor of Virginia, in a suit over the payment of a portion of the Virginia state debt. The West Virginia legislature ignored the decision, and in 1918 Virginia sought a mandamus to compel payment. The Court reserved the matter for further argument, which was never held, as West Virginia later decided to pay the debt and the case ended, fifty-six years after the debt was contracted. There have been a number of instances where states have ignored or refused to accept decisions by lower Federal Courts.

At the conclusion of a review of the record of the Supreme Court in interstate cases, two significant facts stand out. First, the decisions of the Court have usually been accepted, in spite of the fact that the Court has refrained from using armed force; and second, the refusal

[1]See Frank J. Goodnow, Principles of Constitutional Government, p. 33
[2]21 Howard, 506, 512.

of states in rare instances to abide by Court decisions has not resulted in the destruction of the Court's usefulness nor seriously lowered its prestige. It is safe to say, that the Supreme Court was never so well established as at the present time. Indeed, current criticism of it is based chiefly on the ground that it exercises too much, rather than too little, authority.

We have discussed the Supreme Court at such length not because it is a perfect example of the kind of World Court which is needed, but because its experience does demonstrate conclusively that military sanctions are not essential to the successful functioning of such an institution. In the light of this experience, let us examine more in detail the non-military sanctions available for international agencies.

INTERNATIONAL SANCTIONS

It is well to remind ourselves in the beginning that there is no way to *guarantee* international security. There are, however, several measures available which afford the nations reasonable protection. The first factor in the enforcement of international awards is the agreement of the peoples and governments of the various nations to abide by the decisions of such international agencies as they have created and authorized to deal with carefully specified problems. "When nations agree to submit to a tribunal," says former Secretary Hughes, "and to abide by the decision, its observance is a point of international honor of the highest sort. You can really have no better sanction than this and the obligation is one which will be all the more keenly felt when the decision is not simply that of a temporary arbitral tribunal, but of a permanent court supported by practically all the nations of the world."[1] Governments usually keep their

[1] Washington Speech, April 27, 1923.

promises. Broken agreements are the exception, not the rule. Cynicism and suspicion with regard to the integrity of other peoples and governments are major obstacles to international cooperation. Faith and trust are just as essential in international relations as in every other sphere of life. In spite of numerous historic examples of broken treaties and unfulfilled promises by the various nations, it is down the pathway of mutual trust and confidence that the peoples of the earth must proceed if the goal of peace and justice is ever to be attained.

A second factor in enforcement is the enormous power of public opinion. In addressing the delegates of the Conference on the Cause and Cure of War, President Coolidge said: "I feel strongly that public opinion, based on proper information, working through agencies that the common man may see and understand, may be made the ultimate authority among the nations . . . As the cornerstone of such a system would stand an international tribunal whose character and abilities would deserve and retain confidence. Such a tribunal would rely for the enforcement of its decrees, not upon armies and fleets and all the related means of destruction, but rather upon the two most constructive forces in the world. These two forces have lifted society to its present level of civilization . . . These two forces are the intelligence of the mass of individuals and the moral opinion of the community. It is not thinkable that these forces are available and adequate to maintain order within the limits of a great state or nation and yet incapable of adaptation to the international, intergovernmental differences which grow into the causes of war. Nor is it believable that a world-wide public opinion which frowned upon war would be defied by any nation, however powerful. The interdependence of peoples and nations becomes more marked with every year. None can stand alone. None dares court isolation. None may risk the ill opinion of civilization."

Individuals, groups and nations are alike sensitive to the approval and disapproval of their fellows. The successful application of moral condemnation to a recalcitrant nation, however, depends upon a relative difference in degree of guilt on the part of the powers concerned. For the kettle to call the pot black is not likely to be an effective way of producing penitence and a change of action. On the other hand, those nations that have achieved a reputation for equitable dealings are in a position to exert a very powerful moral influence on other peoples.

A third measure in enforcement is diplomatic pressure. The nations are now so interdependent and have such varied and important contacts that the severance of diplomatic relations is a matter of very great significance. If the member nations of an international agency should jointly sever diplomatic relations with a recalcitrant power until it had fulfilled an international agreement or accepted a judicial or arbitral award, the consequences would be exceedingly serious for such a country. The prolongation of a diplomatic boycott would produce such serious consequences for the lawless nation that a heavy premium would be placed upon acceptance of the decisions of international agencies. Indeed, if it were known in advance that a considerable majority of member nations would coöperate in enforcing an international award by instituting a diplomatic boycott and by refusing to have any official dealings whatever with the recalcitrant power until acceptance, this fact in itself would prove sufficient to prevent aggression, in all but extreme cases.

A fourth measure in enforcement available as a last resort is an economic boycott by member nations against a lawless power. The difference between an economic *blockade* and an economic *boycott* should be emphasized. The former requires armed force and if successfully applied means the forcible prevention of food and other basic necessities from entering the blockaded country. Such a procedure in fact has many of the characteristics of war, so much so that the present writer finds himself unable to justify it on ethical grounds. On the other hand, an economic boycott, while it is an extreme form of ostracism, does not involve the use of armed force against another nation. All that is required is that the various governments participating in the boycott should refuse to give clearance papers or other official documents required in international commerce to traders with the offending nation.

The Shotwell-Bliss plan of Disarmament and Security submitted to the League contains an article dealing with this point, as follows: "In the event of any High Contracting Party having been adjudged an aggressor pursuant to this Treaty, all commercial, trade, financial and property interests of the aggressor and of its nationals shall cease to be entitled, either in the territories of the other signatories or on the high seas, to any privileges, protection, rights or immunities accorded by either international law, national law or treaty. Any High Contracting Party may in such case take such other steps toward the severance of trade, financial, commercial and personal intercourse with the aggressor and its nationals as it may deem proper and the H.C.P. may also consult together in this regard." In commenting upon this article, Professor Shotwell says: "This is the heart of the whole treaty. For the first time in international law, we have a method of treaty enforcement which both leaves the H.C.P. free to apply the enforcement or not, as they see fit, and yet, at the same time, secures an enforcement that is real and adequate. . . . In a word, the aggressor is outlawed, and, as such deprived of any security for his property in other lands. Automatically he loses his own security throughout the whole world."[1]

[1]A Practical Plan for Disarmament, pp. 344, 354, 355. This very important publication can be secured for five cents from the Carnegie Endowment For International Peace, 407 W. 117 St., New York City.

The moral phase of an economic boycott is decidedly different from that of an economic blockade. In the former case the nations simply say: "We will have no dealings with you until you fulfil the conditions of membership in the family of nations." There is an obvious ethical difference in a policy of non-cooperation or boycott, like that of Gandhi and his followers on the one hand, and an armed blockade, like that of the Allies against Germany, on the other. Another advantage of using the economic boycott is that it may be applied in varying degrees. It may be executed in such a way as to avoid the danger of starving a boycotted people, and yet in a manner calculated to bring a lawless government to terms. It must be admitted, however, that a universal boycott rigidly enforced would have the same consequences as a blockade. Thus the writer is unable to justify a boycott to the extent of starving recalcitrant peoples. If a partial boycott were enforced against a nation, such a power would sooner or later be compelled to fulfill the conditions necessary for the removal of the embargo. Indeed the mere threat of such a boycott would prove to be an exceedingly powerful deterrent to any aggressive government.

A fifth factor in the enforcement of international awards is *patience*—patience to endure humiliation and loss if necessary while non-military sanctions are securing the desired results. In most realms of life the need for patience is readily recognized. In no sphere is it more needed than in international relations. It is far better that an international agency should have its decisions ignored temporarily, as has been the case with the Supreme Court of the United States on several occasions, than to run the risk of precipitating a general war by resorting to armed sanctions.

What then shall we say concerning the sanctions available for use by duly constituted international agencies? We have shown the enormous difficulty, if not absolute impossibility, of assembling a genuinely international police force, under the conditions which seem certain to prevail throughout the lifetime of this generation, and the equally difficult task of securing the unanimity of action on the part of the various nations required for its effective use in disputes of great significance, and have pointed out that such an attempt might easily precipitate a general war among the nations. We have called attention to the very great difference between using force against individual criminals or small groups of law-breakers and of using armed force against an organized social body such as a nation. The available evidence seems to the writer to be conclusive that the use of mass force against millions of people, including innocent as well as guilty, is ineffective and unethical, and may prove to be suicidal for all involved if again used on a great scale.

On the other hand, effective non-military sanctions are available for use by international agencies, including (1) the agreement of peoples and governments to abide by duly authorized judicial and arbitral awards; (2) the moral power of aroused and intelligent public opinion; (3) diplomatic pressure and the diplomatic boycott; (4) in flagrant cases the economic boycott; (5) patience.

It is readily admitted that these measures do not *guarantee* the fulfillment of all international obligations or the acceptance of all international judicial or arbitral awards. As a matter of fact there is no conceivable way to guarantee absolutely that nations can always be prevented from acts of gross aggression and grave injustice, or be compelled in every case to make satisfactory restitution. But it does seem to the writer that the evidence is conclusive that the five measures proposed, offer infinitely better safeguards than are furnished by national armaments, an international police or any other measure involving the use of armed forces against millions of people. If security and justice are to be achieved, it seems reasonably certain that we must move in the direction indicated by the foregoing proposals, rather than by perpetuating the armaments system, whether national or international in administration.

CHAPTER III

TO WHAT EXTENT ARE EXISTING
INTERNATIONAL AGENCIES ADEQUATE?

THE HAGUE TRIBUNAL

The establishment of the Hague Tribunal in 1899 marked the high point of the steady advance toward international arbitration during the decades prior to 1914. This Tribunal is a marked improvement on previous efforts in that it provides a permanent panel of arbitrators and outlines a definite method of procedure. It is not a real court of justice, however, having no permanent judges, no regular sessions, no continuity of procedure, and no adequate body of international law upon which to base its decisions. Nevertheless, it has rendered important service in settling disputes which have been voluntarily submitted to it by the nations concerned, and is still available for use.

THE PERMANENT COURT OF INTERNATIONAL JUSTICE

The Covenant of the League of Nations provided for the establishment of the Permanent Court of International Justice. This institution has now been functioning for three years. It seems probable that historians of the future will refer to the founding of this court as the beginning of a new epoch in international relations. At the Second Hague Conference statesmen from various nations advocated the establishment of such a court. Inability to agree upon a method of electing judges was all that prevented the establishment of a permanent international court at that time. Not until the close of the war was another attempt made to establish such a court.

Let us examine briefly the structure and functions of the Permanent Court of International Justice. There are eleven judges and four deputy-judges. The old controversy between the great powers and the small nations concerning the method of electing the judges was overcome by having the election conducted jointly by the Council and the Assembly of the League of Nations, the former being dominated by the great powers and the latter by the small nations. To be elected, a candidate must receive the approval of both bodies. The judges are elected from the eminent jurists of the world without regard to nationality and serve for a term of nine years.

The statute of the court provides that its decisions shall be based upon:[1] (1) International conventions, whether general or particular, establishing rules expressly recognized by the contesting States; (2) international customs, as evidence of a general practice accepted by law; (3) the general principles of law recognized by civilized nations; (4) judicial decisions and the teachings of the most highly qualified publicists of the various nations, as subsidiary means for the determination of rules of law. In spite of much current opinion to the contrary, a considerable body of international law and custom is available for use by the court. In referring to this question, Professor J. W. Garner, of the University of Illinois, says: "There is already a vast body of well-settled law—conventional, customary and judge-made." More than one thousand current international treaties have been registered at Geneva, in addition to numerous agreements reached in a not inconsiderable number of international conferences of various kinds in which the nations were officially represented. "There are more than two thousand adjudicated cases in American courts which have to do with the Law of Nations."[2] Moreover,

---

[1]Article 38.

[2]Philip Marshall Brown, International Society, p. 32.

there are four hundred different international organizations which are seeking to reach international agreements of one kind or another, and which are thereby directly or indirectly aiding in the creation of international law.

The court does not have compulsory jurisdiction, that is, it does not have the right to summon a state before it for trial. The statute of the court does contain a provision, however, whereby any nation may sign what is called the optional clause and thereby accept the compulsory jurisdiction of the court in all legal disputes with other signatories of this clause concerning any question of international law, the interpretation of a treaty, the existence of any fact as to breach of an international obligation, and reparation for such a breach. To date 25 nations, including France, Brazil, Denmark, Sweden and Norway, have signed this optional clause.

The Court protocol was ratified in 1921, the judges were elected in September, 1921, and the first opinion was handed down on July 31, 1922. Within three years from that date five judgments and eleven advisory opinions were given. The judgments have dealt with the freedom of the Kiel Canal, concessions in Palestine, interpretation of the Treaty of Neuilly, and concessions in Jerusalem; while the opinions have dealt with such questions as the nomination of delegates to the International Labor Conference, the competence of the International Labor Organization to deal with conditions of labor of agricultural workers and as to agricultural production, nationality decrees in Tunis and Morocco, dispute between Finland and Russia as to Eastern Carelia, validity of contracts and leases of German settlers in Poland, acquisition of Polish nationality by German settlers, boundary dispute between Poland and Czecho-Slovakia, ownership of a monastery on the Albanian frontier, exchange of Greek and Turkish populations, expulsion of the Greek Patriarch from Constantinople.[1] To what extent is the court, as at present constituted, adequate to meet the needs of the international situation? There seems to be general satisfaction with the present method of selecting the judges, although some important critics have expressed the opinion that it is a dangerous procedure to have judges elected by political bodies like the Council and the Assembly. In this connection attention should be called to the fact that all judges derive their appointment and authority from a political agency of one kind or another. Mr. Elihu Root says: "However perfect may be the distinction between judicial and political powers, the personnel of the judiciary must necessarily have its origin in the political power." There is general agreement that the present court is composed of judges whose eminent qualifications and high character are unquestioned. The present court includes judges from the United States,[2] Great Britain, France, Italy, Japan, Holland, Denmark, Switzerland, Spain, Cuba, Brazil; and deputy-judges from Norway, Roumania, China and Jugo-Slavia.

Concerning the existing body of international law, there are grave deficiencies. Thus far nations have been so jealous of their sovereign rights that they have been very reluctant to enter into international agreements which would restrict their freedom of action. Modern international relations are exceedingly complex and as yet they are inadequately covered by international agreements. In spite of the fact that the increasing interdependence of the nations is compelling the negotiation of a rapidly growing number of international treaties, only a beginning has been made. A considerably enlarged body

[1]For a comprehensive history of the Court, see Manley O. Hudson, The Permanent Court of International Justice.

[2]Professor John Bassett Moore, of Columbia University Law School, was elected Neither he, nor any other judge, serves on the court as the official representative of his country.

of international law is required before the court can really
be effective in serious crises. Moreover, there is urgent
need for the codification of existing international law.
Most international agreements have come about in a
haphazard fashion, with the result that there is much
confusion and uncertainty as to just what law actually
exists.

Specialists in international law are generally agreed that
it is utterly impossible for an international conference to
draft a comprehensive code of international law at one
time.[1] For example, Professor J. W. Garner of the
University of Illinois, says: "In my judgment, those men
and women who believe that it is possible to codify at one
time the whole body of international law are pursuing a
will-of-the-wisp. I do not believe it can be done."[2]
Historic attempts at codification of national laws or even
state laws reveal the enormous difficulties involved and
the long periods of time required for completion. Nevertheless, there are urgent reasons why the codification of
existing international law and the creation of new law
should be carried forward as rapidly as possible. Fortunately this need is being recognized and there is every
likelihood that substantial progress in this direction will
be made within the near future. As is well known, Senator
Borah, Chairman of the Committee on Foreign Relations
of the Senate, has repeatedly urged the calling of an
international conference for the purpose of beginning the
codification of international law. There has been considerable misunderstanding of Senator Borah's proposal.
In some quarters it has been assumed that he is calling
for the complete codification of international law by one
conference, whereas his proposal provides for periodic
conferences to continue the process of codification.

Two important projects looking to the codification of

[1]For a discussion of limited, rather than universal, codification of international law, see Manley O. Hudson's peace plan, in Ways to Peace, p. 295.
[2]Report of the Conference on the Cause and Cure of War, p. 176.

international law have recently been initiated. The first is the report on the Codification of American International Law submitted to the Pan American Union by the American Institute of International Law. The proposals enumerated in this report will be considered by the International Commission of Jurists at its meeting in Rio de Janeiro on August 2, 1926. This commission of jurists was appointed by the Fifth Pan American Conference, held at Santiago, Chile, in 1923. The subject matter included in the projects of the American Institute is very extensive and includes such questions as jurisdiction, international rights and duties, immigration, responsibility of Governments, diplomatic protection, extradition, freedom of transit, navigation of international rivers, aerial navigation, treaties, diplomatic agents, consuls, exchange of publications, interchange of professors and students, maritime neutrality, pacific settlement, Pan American court of justice, measures of repression, conquests.

A second step in the direction of codification is the appointment by the Council of the League of Nations of a special committee, of which former Attorney General Wickersham is a member, to make recommendations concerning those phases of international law which are now sufficiently developed for codification. This committee is at present engaged upon the preparation of its report.[1]

The Permanent Court of International Justice is severely handicapped in its efforts to administer justice and maintain peace not only by the lack of adequate law and the delay in codification, but also by the fact that the institution of war has a legal status in existing international law and that many of the provisions of the law of nations

---

[1] In referring to the importance of the work of such a committee, Professor J. W. Garner, of the University of Illinois, says: "I desire to emphasize the point that the preparatory or preliminary work of codification must be done by a relatively small number of jurists and legal experts. I do not believe that it can be left to a large and unwieldy conference of diplomats and politicians." (Report of the Conference on the Cause and Cure of War, p. 175).

now deal with the rules of war. Before the court can function with maximum effectiveness, the present legal status of war must be abolished and the institution of war must be outlawed as a public crime by a general treaty of the nations. If war between states were legalized in our Federal law, the Supreme Court would be impotent to deal with serious crises between states. For the same reasons the Permanent Court will be unable to function effectively in international crises so long as each nation has the legal right to go to war whenever it so chooses. War between nations must be outlawed by international law, as war between states has already been outlawed by our Federal law.

In this connection it is of great significance that the proposed codification of American international law deals only with the laws of peace. In presenting his report to the Pan American Union, Dr. James Brown Scott, President of the American Institute of International Law, said: "The members were of the opinion that the law of war should find no place in the relations of the American Republics with one another, as war would be—if Pan Americanism is more than a word—little less than civil war . . . The members of the executive committee and of the institute present at Lima were therefore a unit in believing that only the law of peace should be considered, as peace should be, and in fact is, the normal state of affairs."[1] An international treaty outlawing war as a public crime is the only enduring foundation upon which to build international law.

The Permanent Court is also greatly restricted in its usefulness by its lack of compulsory, or as it is sometimes called obligatory or affirmative, jurisdiction. At the present time it is competent to hear only those cases that are voluntarily submitted to it by the parties concerned. The committee of jurists, appointed by the Council of

---

[1] Codification of_American International Law, p. 6.

the League, of which Mr. Elihu Root was a member, recommended that the court be granted compulsory jurisdiction over justiciable questions, but this recommendation was not adopted. The Geneva Protocol for the Pacific Settlement of International Disputes of 1924 also provided for compulsory jurisdiction of the Court, but it is now evident that the protocol will not be ratified. There is general agreement among the eminent jurists of the world that compulsory jurisdiction is essential to the effective functioning of the Court in crises. The proposed plan for a Pan American Court of International Justice calls for compulsory jurisdiction of the Court.

There has been a sharp controversy over the provision of the statute of the Permanent Court which deals with advisory opinions. Senator Borah and others have vigorously attacked this practice on the ground that it is not a legitimate function for a court of law. On the other hand, many specialists in international law look upon the practice of giving advisory opinions not only as a legitimate function but a very necessary one as well. Professor Manley O. Hudson, of Harvard University, has recently called attention to the fact that the giving of advisory opinions is not only the practice of many Canadian, British and Continental Courts, but also of several of our state courts.[1] Since 1781 the Massachusetts Supreme Judicial Court has given 140 advisory opinions. The courts of New Hampshire, Maine, Rhode Island, Florida, Colorado, South Dakota, Delaware and Alabama also give advisory opinions. After commenting in detail upon the procedure followed by the Permanent Court in the advisory opinions already given, Professor Hudson says: "Under these circumstances, it is difficult to see what the advisory opinions of the Permanent Court of International Justice lack to give them the quality of 'judiciality' in the

---

[1] See The Permanent Court of International Justice, by Manley O. Hudson, Chapter 5, for a comprehensive discussion of this whole question.

full sense of that term . . . It is too early to say what
is an appropriate function of the new Court until we watch
the experiment for a time. To date, the indications are
all in its favor."[1]

THE LEAGUE OF NATIONS

The general activities of the League are too well known
to require detailed description at this point.[2] It may help
us in our evaluation, however, if we refresh our minds
briefly concerning the main outlines of the League's procedure and its chief accomplishments to date. The
Council is the executive body of the League, while the
Assembly is an open forum of the nations through which
debate on current international issues is carried on and
through which the attention of the world is directed to
threatening international situations. The Secretariat is
composed of more than 400 permanent officials, drawn
from many nations. There are various commissions, including one on mandates, a permanent armaments commission and a temporary commission on limitation of
armaments. There are sections on finance and economics,
transit and communications, international health, intellectual cooperation, control of opium traffic, suppression
of white slave traffic, protection of minorities, etc. The
League has gathered together an enormous mass of valuable data concerning many phases of international relations. It has assembled a continuous series of international
conferences, some of which have made a real contribution
toward the solution of serious problems. The annual
sessions of the Assembly have served as a meeting place
and conference table for delegates from all parts of the
world. It is difficult to exaggerate the significance of this
constant interchange of ideas in commission meetings,

[1]Ibid, p. 168.
[2]For a description of the activities of the League, see The League of Nations
Year Book, published by the World Peace Foundation, 40 Mt. Vernon St.,
Boston, twenty-five cents; and Irving Fisher, League or War; Irving Fisher,
America's Interest in World Peace.

conferences and assemblies. Representatives of the various nations are becoming better acquainted with each other and are coming to understand more fully the position maintained by other peoples. Nothing could be more significant for the peace of the world than the steady growth of the spirit of cooperation at Geneva. A new diplomacy, based upon sympathetic understanding and friendly cooperation, is slowly and steadily being created. Several ominous international disputes have already been settled by the League and substantial headway is being made in solving other threatening international problems.

At the 1924 session of the Assembly a protocol for the Pacific Settlement of International Disputes was adopted and submitted to the respective nations for ratification. The main provisions of the protocol are as follows: The branding of aggressive war as an international crime; definition of an aggressor nation as one that refuses arbitration or judicial settlement; compulsory jurisdiction of the international court over legal disputes; compulsory arbitration of all other disputes; prevention of hostile preparations for war; demilitarization of certain zones; application of diplomatic, economic and military sanctions against the aggressor; calling an international conference on disarmament. Whatever the shortcomings of this protocol and whatever the dangers inherent in it—and we should not overlook the elements of great menace in some of its provisions—surely it represents an enormous advance over any method of settling international disputes hitherto adopted by any international conference, and will serve as an exceedingly valuable precedent in future efforts to make effective the outlawry of war.

What are the chief weaknesses of the League at present? First, several powerful nations are not included in its membership, notably the United States, Germany and Russia. The League cannot function with maximum effectiveness until it embraces all nations. Second, it lacks adequate jurisdiction and power to deal with many of the most pressing and dangerous international problems. It is in much the same position that our Continental Congress was; whereas in that case power resided in the states and the Congress was a mere shadow, now the nations have retained power and for the most part have refused to recognize the necessity of delegating authority to international agencies to deal with problems which are genuinely international in character and which cannot be solved by national action alone. Third, control of the League is unduly in the hands of the Council, which at present means it is dominated by the victorious allied powers. This weakness would in part be remedied by admitting Germany, Russia and the United States to equal places on the Council. But even if this were done, it would still be advisable to increase the relative power of the Assembly. Fourth, the League as at present constituted rests ultimately on armed force. This appears to the writer to be a source of great potential danger. So far as the use of armed force to compel acceptance of the decisions of international agencies of justice is concerned, Secretary Hughes has well reminded us that when unanimity of action on the part of various nations can be secured there is least need for armed force, and when such unanimity cannot be secured the use of force is least effective. The writer is of the opinion that so long as the League depends ultimately upon contingents from national armies and navies to enforce its decisions, it is building upon sand, perhaps even upon quicksand.

THE INTERNATIONAL LABOR ORGANIZATION

Part XIII of the Versailles Treaty provided for the establishment of the International Labor Organization. For many decades prior to the war the necessity for international labor legislation had been recognized by persons interested in the welfare of workers. Competition is not confined within national boundaries and therefore labor conditions in one country very vitally affect conditions in other lands. Legislation designed for the protection of the workers will be ineffective if it is enacted by one country alone. Therefore periodic attempts have been made for more than half a century to bring about international agreements with regard to working conditions, and at the Paris Exposition in 1900 the International Association for Labor Legislation was formed.[1] At the end of the war the need for a more comprehensive organization was recognized and so the International Labor Organization was founded.

The International Labor Organization holds an annual conference for the consideration of international labor problems and the formation of Draft Conventions which are submitted to the state members or ratification and recommendations. The Conference is composed of four representatives of each state member, of whom two are Government delegates, and the other two delegates representing respectively the employers and the workers. The first conference was held at Washington in October, 1919. Draft conventions dealing with the eight-hour day, unemployment, employment of women before and after childbirth, employment of women during the night, prevention of anthrax, protection against lead poisoning, minimum age of children employed in industry, night work of young people employed in industry.

The second part of the International Labor Organization is the International Labor Office maintained at Geneva. The office is under the control of a Governing Body, composed of representatives of governments, employers' associations and workers' organizations. Some 350 persons representing 30 different nationalities are permanently employed under the supervision of a Director

---

[1] For a comprehensive history of international labor legislation see Bontelle Ellsworth Lowe, The International Protection of Labor, 439 pages.

and Deputy-Director. The members of this staff are gathered from all the leading nations and many of them are highly trained experts in their respective fields. An elaborate research section is constantly gathering information concerning labor problems from all parts of the world. This information is available for use of all who are interested, including delegates to the annual conferences, members of the Office, representatives of Governments, representatives of employers' associations and of workers' organizations, etc.

A number of important commissions have been set up by the Labor Office, including the following: Joint Maritime Commission, Commission on Unemployment, Mixed Advisory Committee on Agriculture, Emigration Commission, Advisory Committee on Anthrax, Advisory Committee on Industrial Hygiene, Conference of Experts on Disablement, Committee of Experts on Social Insurance, Correspondence Committee on Cooperation.

This constant interchange of ideas and information is of very great significance. Out of these conferences and commission meetings are emerging international agreements which will ultimately constitute the foundation of an international code of labor legislation. The chief disappointment of supporters of the Labor Organization thus far has been the long delay in ratification of Draft Conventions by the various nations. Nevertheless, the activities of the Labor Organization are having a most wholesome educational influence throughout the world. Several notable improvements in labor conditions have already resulted from its efforts, and undoubtedly great strides in this direction will be made during the next decade.

CHAPTER IV

WHAT ARE THE CHIEF BARRIERS TO MORE EFFECTIVE INTERNATIONAL ORGANIZATION?

ABSOLUTE NATIONAL SOVEREIGNTY

The first and foremost of these barriers is the prevalence of the doctrine of absolute national sovereignty. "National sovereignty remains inalienable and inviolate," is the first sentence in a resolution passed by the Inter Parliamentary Union at the Hague in 1894. Scores of similar quotations could easily be cited. Mr. Philip Kerr, formerly Private Secretary to Mr. Lloyd George, bears effective testimony at this point: "What is the fundamental cause of war? I do not say the only cause of war, but the most active and constant cause. It is not race, or religion, or color, or nationality, or despotism, or commercial rivalry, or any of the causes usually cited. It is the division of humanity into absolutely separate sovereign states."[1] It is widely assumed that there is not and should not be any law higher than the law of a nation, that no outside agency has a right to interfere with the legitimate activities of a nation, it further being assumed that a nation has the right to determine for itself what activities are legitimate. Therefore, in its extreme form national sovereignty means the right of a nation to do as it pleases, subject only to the possibility that any given right may be disputed with force of arms by another nation. A good example of this attitude is found in a proposed reservation to the League Covenant which received the votes of 36 Senators on November 17, 1919, as follows: "The United States reserves to itself exclusively the right to decide what

[1]The Prevention of War, p. 16.

questions affect its honor or its vital interests . . ."
Needless to say, if all nations rigidly adhered to such a
policy, the inevitable result would be international
anarchy.

This extreme doctrine exists only in theory, because
in practice every nation submits to limitations of absolute
sovereignty. Every treaty that is signed limits the
freedom of action of the signatories, as does every international agreement of any kind. Nevertheless, nations
are exceedingly jealous of their sovereign rights and
look with deep suspicion upon all encroachments upon
their powers of self-determination. Their fear of "super-
government" has made them very reluctant to grant
adequate jurisdiction to international agencies. The
failure of the nations to clothe international agencies
with adequate authority and jurisdiction to deal with
problems which are world-wide in scope, and which
therefore cannot be solved by national action alone, has
to that degree served to perpetuate international anarchy
—lawlessness among nations—which has been the chief
cause of war.

"Some readiness to admit of qualifications of the
asserted absolute sovereignty of the state" says Professor
Edwin Borchard, of Yale University, "must accompany
any plan for the international regulation of the causes of
war. Nations that undertake to constitute themselves
plaintiff, judge and sheriff in their own cause, cannot be
expected to make any serious contribution to the pro-
motion of peace."[1] Former Attorney-General Wickersham
says: "Just so long as a nation is unwilling to subject
itself to some sort of restrictive agreement, just so long
its protestations of love of peace, of willingness to aid
in ridding the world of the terrible scourge of war, amounts
to nothing more than the hollow mockery of empty
promises."

[1]Ways to Peace, p. 55.

The reluctance to extend the sphere of law and orderly processes of justice is of very ancient origin. For an indefinitely long period patriarchs and chieftains were sovereign powers and deeply resented any encroachment upon their prerogatives. In that day a condition of anarchy prevailed between the various patriarchs. In other ages sovereignty resided in cities; every city was a law unto itself, and all efforts to establish inter-city agencies of justice were vigorously resisted by advocates of city sovereignty. The citizens of London on a famous occasion cried out: "We will have no king but the Mayor."[1]

For several centuries numberless feudal states throughout Europe were governed by petty rulers who claimed and frequently exercised absolute sovereignty. In that day national government was regarded as "super-government" and was strenuously opposed by barons and petty kings. The strong opposition in many quarters to the creation of our Federal government is also well known. The Articles of Confederation declared that "each State retains its sovereignty, freedom and independence." So jealous were the states of their sovereign rights that even during the dangerous days of the Revolutionary War they refused to grant adequate authority to the Continental Congress. Finally, at the conclusion of the war, the Continental Congress became almost wholly impotent due to the low esteem in which it was held by the states and to the fact that they would neither grant it adequate jurisdiction nor respond to its appeals. In the Constitutional Convention a long and bitter fight was waged by advocates of state sovereignty against the formation of a Federal Union which would seriously abridge the sovereign rights of the states.[2] It was

---

[1]Hugo Krabbe, The Modern Idea of the State, p. XVII.

[2]For a comprehensive history of this struggle, see James Madison's Notes of Debates in the Federal Convention of 1787, edited by James Brown Scott; and Jonathan Elliott, Debates in the Several State Conventions on the Adoption of the Federal Constitution, 5 volumes.

regarded as unwise to publish the record of the debates in the Constitutional Convention until 50 years later. The reason is indicated in James Madison's notes: "Mr. King suggested that the Journal of the Convention should be either destroyed, or deposited in the custody of the President. He thought if suffered to be made public, a bad use would be made of them by those who would wish to prevent the adoption of the Constitution."[1]

Patrick Henry—of "Give me liberty, or give me death" fame—was one of the leaders of the struggle to preserve unimpaired the sovereignty of the states. In the Virginia Convention called to consider the ratification of the Constitution, Mr. Henry made speeches on seventeen of the twenty-two days of its duration, speaking from three to eight times per day, and on one occasion being on his feet for seven hours. Listen to the vigorous words he used in attacking the proposed Federal Government: "We are come hither to preserve the poor Commonwealth of Virginia, if it can be done: something must be done to preserve your liberty and mine . . . This Constitution is said to have beautiful features; but when I come to examine these features, sir, they appear to me horribly frightful. Among other deformities, it has an awful squinting; it squints toward monarchy. . . Your President may easily become king . . . I would rather infinitely, and I am sure most of this Convention are of the same opinion, have a king, lords, and commons, than a government so replete with such insupportable evils. . . . As this government stands, I despise and abhor it. . . . I have, I fear, fatigued the Committee; yet I have not said the one hundred thousandth part of what I have on my mind, and wish to impart."[2]

In the New York Convention, Mr. Tredwell said: "This government is founded in sin, and reared up in

[1]The Debates in the Federal Conventions of 1787, edited by Gaillard Hunt and James Brown Scott, p. 582.
[2]Elliott, Vol. 3, pp. 45, 46, 58, 59, 546.

iniquity . . . If it goes into operation, we shall be greatly punished with the total extinction of our civil liberties."[1] In several states ratification of the Constitution was secured by a very narrow margin; in Virginia the vote was yeas 89, nays 79; in New York, yeas 30, nays 27; in Rhode Island yeas 34, nays 32; in Massachusetts yeas 187, nays 168; in New Hampshire yeas 57, nays 46.[2] Woodrow Wilson pointed out that "two of the thirteen states held aloof from the Union until they could be assured of its stability and success; many of the other states had come into reluctantly, all with a keen sense of sacrifice."[3]

The doctrine of absolute sovereignty has always been the foe of law and order. Between sovereign entities, each exercising the right to do as it pleases, a condition of anarchy prevails, whether the sovereign entities be tribes, cities, feudal states, states, or nations. Progress in extending the sphere of law and order has been made possible only by the voluntary relinquishment of certain sovereign rights. If Patrick Henry and those of like point of view had prevailed, the creation of an effective Federal Government would have been rendered impossible. And so today the chief foes of effective international agencies are the extreme advocates of national sovereignty. Real freedom for the states was made more secure by the creation of interstate government, and real freedom for the nations can be maintained only by strengthening international agencies of justice.

Analogies are always dangerous and should never be pressed too far. Very few students of world problems believe that it is possible or advisable to create a world government with powers over the nations analogous to the powers of our Federal Government over the states. So long as nationalism prevails it will be necessary to have

[1]Ibid, Vol. 2, p. 405.
[2]World Almanac, 1925 edition, p. 227.
[3]Congressional Government, p. 18.

international agreements ratified by the various nations
before they become operative. The urgent need of the
hour is that nations should be willing to gather around
the conference table and, after full and frank discussion,
formulate cooperative solutions of mutual problems, and
then be willing to ratify and abide by such international
agreements, even at the expense of diminishing national
freedom of action. In this way all that is valuable in
national sovereignty may be preserved, and yet without
constituting an insurmountable barrier to international
peace and justice.

NATIONAL ARMAMENTS

The second great obstacle to more effective international organization is the maintenance of national
armaments. Continuous support for a program of military
preparedness can be maintained only by appealing to the
fears of the voters. The creation of this fear requires a
very elaborate propaganda against the people of other
nations. Propaganda designed for the purpose of engen-
dering fear has three vicious results: (1) It brings about
suspicion, misunderstanding and hostility between peoples,
and thereby destroys the basis of mutual sympathy and
trust, without which effective international cooperation
is impossible; (2) propaganda of this character tends to
deceive peoples into believing that military preparedness
furnishes adequate security and that, therefore, international agencies are not really essential; (3) moreover, such
propaganda minimizes the effectiveness of international
organization as a method of maintaining peace and justice,
and derision is heaped upon non-military means of achieving security against aggression.

Rear Admiral Fiske, of the United States Navy, before
a very influential audience, recently said: "International
law is not law at all; and incalculable harm has been done
to our national security by those jurists and statesmen

who have made the people believe that it is. The plain fact is that international law is largely international humbug."[1]

Rear Admiral William L. Rodgers, also of the United States Navy, has recently given us another sample of the line of argument advanced by the military mind: "The popular suggestion for securing peace is by means of treaties, international conferences and world courts and other diplomatic and economic agreements, which endeavor to anticipate points of friction and by some pre-existing code of rules provide for their decision when they occur. It is the hope that the existing rule will be observed in time of great national emotion when people are so moved that they contemplate war. It is a vain hope. We all know that great collective emotions are only restrained by force, not reason . . . While international arbitral courts can do much to remove minor causes of international friction, it is almost hopeless for us to look for a Permanent Court of International Justice to bestow peace on the world by judicial procedure . . . A balance of power of the great nations will be the best preservative of peace, with the United States placing a heavy hand in the balance on the side of peace, and the weight of her hand in the balance will depend upon the strength of her army and navy."[2]

The net result, therefore, of the effort to gain support for armaments by creating fear is to make people suspicious and distrustful of each other, to magnify the protection afforded by armies and navies, and to minimize the place of international organization in achieving security.

Fortunately, the inadequacy of military force and the necessity for international cooperation are rapidly being realized. No better illustration of this fact could be found than the change in sentiment in France within the past

---

[1]Annals of the American Academy, July 1925, p. 78.
[2]Ibid, pp. 71-76.

three years. During the Peace Conference and immediately thereafter there was general agreement in France that security could be maintained only by the disarmament of Germany and the military preparedness of France. In spite of the fact that Germany's army has been reduced to 100,000 men and that since the war France has had a degree of military predominance on the continent not equalled by that of any power for a century, and the further fact that France has entered into a series of military alliances with Germany's enemies, in spite of this military prowess, the feeling of insecurity in France has steadily deepened. Confidence in Poincare's policy of military domination by France has been severely shaken. Within the past year France has become one of the foremost advocates of the League of Nations, and is the only great power that has signed the optional clause of the Permanent Court, thereby accepting the compulsory jurisdiction of the Court. French statesmen and peoples alike were bitterly disappointed over the failure of the Geneva Protocol to receive ratification. Now that the protocol has been killed chief interest centers in the pending negotiations for a Four Power Pact between France, Great Britain, Belgium and Germany.[1] If this pact is signed its chief significance will be that the additional security afforded will probably pave the way for an

---

[1]The present negotiations had their origin in an offer from Germany, the chief provisions being:

1. The repudiation of war as a means of settling differences between herself and either her western or eastern neighbors;

2. Unqualified acceptance of her frontiers in the west as fixed by the Treaty of Versailles, thus relinquishing all hope of recovering Alsace-Lorraine.

3. Acceptance of the Treaty obligations covering the perpetual demilitarization of the left bank of the Rhine;

4. That a way be left open either through arbitration, mediation or the League of Nations to reconsider her Eastern frontiers,

5. General arbitration treaties with all her neighbors, guaranteeing a peaceful settlement of all judicial and political differences. (Foreign Policy Association News Bulletin, June 26, 1925).

international conference on reduction of armaments. With the progressive disarmament of the nations assured, the practice of cooperation between the nations will increase, and the prestige and influence of international agencies will rise steadily. If the thirteen states had continued to maintain armaments designed for use against each other, our Federal government would have been fatally handicapped. For the same reasons, the maintenance of large armies and navies will, so long as continued, prevent international agencies from functioning effectively in times of crises. Fortunately, there is some indication that trust in military preparedness is diminishing, whereas confidence in international cooperation is steadily gaining ground.

The United States is in a position to make a very important contribution to the movement for disarmament. We are favored with greater natural security than that possessed by any other great nation, with an ocean on either side and with no actual enemies near or far. President Coolidge, in his address to the graduating class at Annapolis in June, said: "I feel that the occasion will very seldom arise, and I know it does not now exist when those connected with our navy are justified, either directly or by inference, in asserting that other specified Powers are arming against us, and by arousing national suspicion and hatred attempting to cause us to arm against them." Because of our greater degree of security and because of our potential influence in international affairs due to our size and wealth, we should take the initiative in the movement for general disarmament and should set the example by a progressive reduction in our own armaments.

NATURAL DIFFICULTIES

A third great barrier to more effective international organization is constituted by a group of natural difficulties centering around language, race, culture, distances involved, number of people concerned, and the extreme complexity of the problems requiring solution. The language difficulty alone is a very serious one whenever representatives from some fifty nations gather together to consider mutual problems. To convey ideas accurately is a difficult procedure even when all parties involved speak a common tongue; the difficulties are immeasurably greater when translation into two or three languages is necessary. The enormous differences in racial and cultural background represented in an international conference are factors of primary importance. The size of the units represented in such a gathering in itself confronts statesmen with very grave difficulties. To attempt to represent thousands of people of one race and language is a serious undertaking; much more so is the attempt to speak for and on behalf of many millions of diverse peoples. Even with modern means of communication and transportation available, the problem of distance greatly delays speedy action in international undertakings, and finally, the very complexity of modern life makes unavoidable a vast amount of confusion and bewilderment on the part of international statesmen. Even where the spirit of mutual cooperation is fully present, the finding of adequate solutions for the complex and threatening problems of international relations is an exceedingly difficult undertaking. The building of effective international organization in a world of intense nationalism, huge armaments and natural difficulties arising out of differences of language, race, culture, in addition to difficulties inherent in dealing with great distances, vast numbers and infinite complexity, is as gigantic a task as has ever confronted any generation of people.

Chapter V

WHAT SHALL THE UNITED STATES DO ABOUT INTERNATIONAL ORGANIZATION?

That the peoples of the various nations are becoming more and more interdependent and are less and less able to live apart from each other is admitted by all serious students of international affairs. Even a great nation like the United States, with an extraordinarily favorable geographical location, blessed with enormous quantities of essential natural resources, and with vast numbers of energetic and highly skilled citizens, cannot maintain a policy of isolation. This fact was pointed out by President Coolidge in his Chicago address of December 4, 1924: "I am profoundly impressed," he said, "with the fact that the structure of modern society is essentially a unity, destined to stand or fall as such. . . . If we could not avoid involvement in a war whose causes were foreign, and whose issues were chiefly alien to us because we had settled them for ourselves long ago, how can we hope to avoid our full share of responsibility in connection with other world problems which, if they are ever to be solved, must be solved in an atmosphere of peace and good-will?"

For a powerful nation like the United States not only to refuse to cooperate in creating effective international agencies, but to manifest downright antagonism to such efforts would prove to be nothing less than a calamity to the cause of world peace. On the other hand, the United States is in a position to render an incalcuable contribution to international security and justice. With vast economic and financial resources, with no traditional hatreds, with less reason to be afraid because of the protection afforded by an ocean on either side, with no actual enemies near or far, with great reserves of moral enthusiam, with all these advantages the United States could easily turn the tide against international anarchy and war and in favor of international organization for the settlement of dispute on a basis of law and fair dealing if—if only she would enter freely and whole-heartedly into cooperation with other nations to this end. With such vast issues at stake, let us consider the steps which should be taken by the United States within the near future.

WORLD COURT

First, the United States should enter the Permanent Court of International Justice without delay. There are differences of opinion concerning the reservations which should be attached to our adherence to the court. The really important thing is that we should actually enter the court with such reservations as are deemed necessary and will be acceptable to the other nations—and thus demonstrate by concrete action that we intend to assume our full share of responsibility for strengthening international agencies of justice. In subsequent paragraphs we shall discuss certain reservations that have recently been proposed by a group of peace advocates.

OUTLAWRY OF WAR

Second, the United States should cooperate fully with all efforts to secure an international treaty outlawing war by declaring it to be a public crime. There are differences of opinion as to the most effective means of accomplishing this end; some persons advocate the calling of a special international conference for this purpose, while others believe that the League of Nations is the agency through which such an agreement could most effectively be negotiated. The all-important consideration is that the peoples and governments of the earth should have the will to outlaw war as a crime and should use their best intelligence as to the most effective way to accomplish this end. The people of the United States, therefore, should insist that

our Government be ready at all times to cooperate fully
with every international endeavor to outlaw war. More
than this, the United States should assume the initiative
in seeking to bring about such an international agreement,
being willing at all times to counsel with representatives
of other nations concerning the most effective way to
accomplish this end.

THE NEW HARMONY PEACE PROGRAM FOR AMERICA

Two immediate steps before the United States, therefore, are, entrance into the world court and cooperation
in an international endeavor to outlaw war. A recent
proposal advanced by an important group of peace
advocates seeks to accomplish both of these ends by
one procedure, namely, that the United States should
enter the court without delay but that continuance in
the court beyond five years should be conditioned upon
the negotiation of an international agreement outlawing
war. This proposal is as follows:

"As a measure directed toward the abolition of war
and in order to make the Permanent Court of International Justice a more effective judicial substitute for
war in the settlement of international disputes, we favor
the program embodied in the three following proposals:

"1. The immediate adherence of the United States
to the Court Protocol, with the Harding-Hughes-
Coolidge reservations.

"2. Within two years after the adherence by the
United States to the Court Protocol, the signatories
thereto, including the United States Government, shall
formally declare by appropriate governmental action
their endorsement of the following basic principles of
the outlawry of war and shall call an international conference of all civilized nations for the purpose of making
a general treaty embodying these principles.

"(a) War between nations shall be outlawed as an

62   AN AMERICAN PEACE POLICY

institution for the settlement of international controversies by making it a crime under the law of nations.
(The question of self-defense against attack or invasion
is not involved or affected.)

"(b) A code of the international law of peace, based
upon the outlawing of war and upon equality and justice
between all nations, great and small, shall be formulated
and adopted.

"(c) When war is outlawed the Permanent Court of
International Justice shall be granted affirmative jurisdiction over international controversies between sovereign nations as provided for and defined in the code
and arising under treaties.

"3. Should such signatories within two years after
the adherence of the United States fail to make such
declaration and to join in a conference for the purpose of
making such general treaty, the United States may in
its discretion withdraw its adherence to said Court
Protocol; and further should such signatories fail,
within five years after the adherence of the United
States to said Court Protocol, to make and execute a
general treaty embodying in substance the aforesaid
principles, the adherence of the United States shall
thereupon terminate; but any action of the court taken
in the interim shall remain in full force and effect."[1]

[1]The following explanatory statement was attached to the foregoing proposal:
"The undersigned persons, representing various points of view as to the
means of securing international peace, agree to the following principles in the
attached program for the outlawry of the institution of war in the adherence
of the United States to the World Court Protocol and agree to devote their
best efforts to its realization and to the further study of adequate and appropriate mechanism for its effective application.

"It is understood that each person signing this program commits only
himself personally to its approval and that he is not limiting in any degree or
manner his freedom to advocate methods or agencies for promoting world peace
other than or additional to the Permanent Court of International Justice.
However, we recognize that the question of the adherence of the United States
to the Protocol of the World Court constitutes the chief immediate issue before
this country, and that it is of paramount importance to bring about the cooperation of the United States with the rest of the world in effective measures
to end war."

The signatories to this agreement are:

Florence E. Allen, Justice of the Ohio Supreme Court.

Bruce Bliven, Associate Editor New Republic; formerly editor New York Globe.

Charles H. Brent, Bishop, Protestant Episcopal Church, Buffalo; formerly Senior Chaplain with the A. E. F. in France.

E. C. Carter, Executive Secretary the Inquiry; formerly Senior Secretary of the Y.M.C.A. with the A.E.F. in France.

John H. Clarke, former Justice of the Supreme Court of the United States.

Donald J. Cowling, President, Carleton College.

Herbert Croly, Editor, New Republic.

Mary Dreier, Executive Board, National Women's Trade Union League.

Edward Mead Earle, Professor at Columbia University.

Sherwood Eddy, National Council of the Y.M.C.A.

William B. Hale, Attorney, Chicago.

Carlton J. H. Hayes, Professor at Columbia University.

John Haynes Holmes, Pastor, Community Church, New York.

F. Ernest Johnson, Secretary, Federal Council of Churches.

Paul Jones, Bishop, Protestant Episcopal Church.

Mrs. B. F. Langworthy, President, Woman's City Club, Chicago.

S. O. Levinson, Chairman, American Committee for the Outlawry of War.

Halford E. Luccock, Contributing Editor of the Christian Advocates.

Julian W. Mack, Judge, United States Circuit Court.

Charles Clayton Morrison, Editor, the Christian Century.

Reinhold Niebuhr, Pastor, Bethel Evangelical Church, Detroit.

Kirby Page, New York City.

Raymond Robins, Chicago.

John A. Ryan, Director, Social Action Department National Catholic Welfare Conference.

John Nevin Sayre, Secretary, Fellowship of Reconciliation.

Professor James T. Shotwell, Director Carnegie Endowment for International Peace, and Co-author of the American Plan for Security and Disarmament submitted to the League Assembly in 1924.

Fred B. Smith, Federal Council of Churches.

Norman Thomas, Director, League for Industrial Democracy.

Wilbur Thomas, American Friends Service Committee, Philadelphia.

William Allen White, Editor, The Emporia Gazette.

Is this agreement a practicable proposal or merely a Utopian dream? The following comment from a recent editorial in a religious journal reveals an attitude which is widely held: "It is fantastic to believe that the nations of the world can be persuaded in five years to 'outlaw war' in any thoroughgoing and substantial way that would mean anything on earth other than a fascinating phrase. Only the most imaginative optimism could possibly hope to accomplish in so very short a time a task of such vast and inconceivably intricate and difficult proportions." This editorial, like many other current comments, fails to distinguish between the *outlawry* of war and the *abolition* of war. The former is only a step in the direction of the latter. An international treaty declaring war to be a public crime will no more abolish international violence than laws against murder have abolished all killing of one individual by another. There is general agreement, however, that the negotiation of an international treaty outlawing war would constitute an enormous stride toward peace. Is there any substantial basis for hope that such an international agreement can be secured within the near future? There are many indications that the nations of Europe are moving rapidly in this direction. The Assembly of the League of Nations in September, 1923, approved and recommended to the nations for adoption the Treaty of Mutual Assistance, Article One of which begins as follows: "The High Contracting Parties solemnly declare that *aggressive war is an international crime* and severally undertake that no one of them will be guilty of its commission." The preamble of the Protocol for the Pacific Settlement of International Disputes adopted at Geneva in 1924 begins as follows: "Animated by the firm desire to ensure the maintenance of general peace and the security of nations whose existence, independence or territories may be threatened; recognizing the solidarity of the members of the international community; asserting that *a war of aggression constitutes a violation of this solidarity and an international crime.*" It is true that the Treaty of Mutual Assistance and the Protocol failed of ratification by the respective nations. Nevertheless there was general agreement concerning the outlawing of aggressive war. The fact that two successive Assemblies branded aggressive war as an international crime establishes a precedent which is not likely to be ignored by future international conferences, and ultimately this idea will be embodied in an international treaty. The German offer of February, 1925, proposes that the signatory nations to a security pact should outlaw war between themselves.

Supporters of the outlawry movement in the United States have frequently insisted that the kind of outlawry proposed by the Treaty of Mutual Assistance and by the Geneva Protocol is not a genuine outlawry proposal, since *defensive* war is sanctioned and provision made for common military action against an aggressor nation. On the other

hand, critics of the American outlawry plan contend that
it does not call for the outlawry of *all* war, since "the
right of defense against actual invasion" is specifically
reserved. One critic insists that this reservation "dis-
embowels the whole plan" for the reason that what is
outlawed "is a kind of war that no nation ever fights—
or at least ever admits that it is fighting. No matter
what the facts may be, no nation ever openly wages an
offensive war." The outlawry advocates respond that
what they propose to outlaw is the *institution* of war, and
that defensive measures against an invader do not constitute war, any more than killing in self-defense by an
individual constitutes murder. In spite of the long
standing controversy, it may be that the gulf between
these two interpretations of outlawry is not so wide as is
supposed by advocates on both sides. Both groups are
endeavoring to secure an international agreement declaring
that an aggressive attack upon another nation is an
international crime, both advocate the continued maintenance of national troops for defensive purposes, both
reserve the right to use these armed forces to repel an
actual invasion, thus it is obvious that neither side is
making a pacifist proposal to refrain altogether from using
armed forces to repel an attack.[1] The chief difference
between the two positions is that outlawry advocates
would provide for armed defense against an aggressor by
national troops alone, or at least without previous military
alliances, whereas supporters of the Protocol regard
definite commitments of *mutual assistance* on the part of
attacked powers as necessary to effective defense against
an aggressor. Thus it is evident that what one side means
by outlawing the *institution* of war is substantially the

---

[1] It should be pointed out, however, that many advocates of outlawry,
including the writer, do not believe that the use of military or naval weapons
against another nation is ever justifiable. For a detailed exposition of this
position see the writer's "War: Its Causes, Consequences and Cure," and "The
Abolition of War."

same as what the other side means by outlawing *aggressive* war. Since both sides insist upon the right of defense against attack, the definition of an aggressor nation becomes all-important. There are numerous historic examples that reveal the grave difficulties involved in determining which nation is the aggressor. Thus far American advocates of outlawry have failed to provide an adequate definition of aggression. The Geneva Protocol, as is well known, made substantial progress in this direction.[1]

While there are serious differences of opinion between the two groups with regard to ways and means of making effective an international outlawry agreement, the important thing about the joint proposal under discussion is that all signatories agree that the making of war an international crime is a necessary step toward its total abolition. In view of the fact that the Assembly has twice branded war as an international crime and that serious efforts are now being put forth to embody this idea in an international treaty, do we not have reason to believe that the first proposal of the joint agreement is really within the realm of practical achievement?

What shall we say concerning the proposal with regard to the codification of international law? It should be recalled that the committee of jurists appointed to draft a plan for the Permanent Court, of which Mr. Root was a member, recommended that an international conference be called to consider the codification of the law of nations. The recommendation was not accepted, but after a long delay the League has taken the beginning steps in the process of codification by appointing a committee of jurists, of which former Attorney General Wickersham is a member, to consider the phases of international law which can most readily be codified. A second important

---

[1]See Protocol for the Pacific Settlement of International Disputes, published by Carnegie Endowment for International Peace, 407 W. 117 St., New York City, price five cents.

move in the direction of codification is the preparation of draft conventions by the American Institute of International Law for consideration by the International Commission of Jurists, when it meets in Rio de Janeiro, in August, 1926. Thus we see that two important efforts are now being made to codify international law. There is room for legitimate difference of opinion as to just how much progress could be made in a single international conference. Supporters of the American plan of outlawry and advocates of the League are alike agreed, however, that new international law should be enacted and that a constantly recurring series of international conferences will be required if codification is to be kept up to date. Some persons believe it advisable to call special conferences for this purpose, while others look upon the League of Nations as the most effective agency through which codification can be achieved. It is important to note, however, that all parties concerned are agreed as to the necessity of codifying existing international law and of creating new law, and all admit that many conferences, not one, will be required before a fully adequate basis of law is available for use by international agencies. Is there not ample reason, therefore, for believing that the gradual codification of international law is practicable?

What about affirmative jurisdiction of the World Court? Is this an impracticable proposal? Here also it should be remembered that the committee of jurists recommended that the Permanent Court be granted obligatory jurisdiction over certain specified cases. While the recommendation was not accepted by the League, provision was made whereby nations could voluntarily accept compulsory jurisdiction of the Court by signing the optional clause. Twenty-five nations, including France, have already signed the optional clause. The Geneva Procotol provided for obligatory jurisdiction of the Court. Moreover this feature is being incorporated in the security pact which is now being negotiated between Germany, France, Great Britain and Belgium. Prominent American jurists have long advocated the granting of compulsory jurisdiction over justiciable questions to an international court. The draft conventions for the codification of American International Law clothe the Pan American Court of International Justice with obligatory jurisdiction. It should be noted carefully that the proposal under discussion does *not* call for compulsory jurisdiction over *all* international questions; compulsory jurisdiction being confined to controversies "provided for and defined in the code and arising under treaties," that is to say, justiciable questions. Even this measure of compulsory jurisdiction does not become operative until war has been outlawed. In the light of these facts, do we not have reason for believing that the governments of the world, including our own, will accept the affirmative jurisdiction of the World Court?

With regard to the provision limiting the adherence of the United States to the Court to a period of five years unless a general treaty embodying the outlawry principles is negotiated, Professor Shotwell has called attention to the fact that there are many precedents for such a reservation. As a matter of fact it is easy to exaggerate the importance of this provision. It is generally admitted, even by persons strongly opposed to entering the Court as at present constituted, that *if the United States once enters the Court there is very little prospect that she will ever actually withdraw.* If at the end of five years the specific conditions have not been fully met, it would be a simple matter for our Government to extend the period of our adherence. For this reason it might be advisable to call attention to this possibility by adding, after the word "terminate" in next to the last line, some such phrase as: "unless provision for an extension of time is made by the United States Government."

For the United States to enter the court immediately, with an endorsement of the proposal to outlaw war by international treaty and with an expression of willingness to accept affirmative jurisdiction when war is outlawed, would be ten-fold more significant than to enter merely on a basis of the Harding-Hughes-Coolidge reservations. If the United States should take such action it would enormously strengthen peace efforts in Europe. Moreover, if an international treaty outlawing war is negotiated, *there is every reason to believe that the United States would join the League of Nations without further delay.* In this connection a recent utterance by the Editor of *The Christian Century,* hitherto a vigorous antagonist of American entrance into the Court or the League, is significant enough to be quoted: "With war outlawed not only the Court but the League of Nations takes on a fundamentally different character. It would be hard to conjure up from the deepest abyss of prejudice and partisanship a single reason for the United States to refuse to enter the League when war has been plucked out of it by the members of the League uniting to make war a crime. We seem, therefore, to have here a proposal which opens a great vista of international cooperation. No one can prophesy how far the nations may go in the pursuit of peace and brotherhood when once they have been released by their own mutual oath from the fear and torment of war."

The stakes are indeed high: Immediate entrance into the Court; cooperation on the part of the United States with other nations in the effort to reach an international agreement outlawing war; speedy entrance into the League by the United States and the assumption of full responsibility for strengthening all international agencies necessary to the maintenance of security and justice. A proposal with such potentialities should not be abandoned until every possibility of its realization has been exhausted.

LEAGUE OF NATIONS

We have suggested two immediate steps which should be taken by the United States—entrance into the World Court, either on a basis merely of the Harding-Hughes-Coolidge reservations or far more preferably on a basis of the joint proposal; and cooperation with all efforts to secure an international agreement outlawing war as a crime, either by calling a special international conference for this purpose, or by cooperating with the efforts of the League of Nations toward this end. A third immediate step is to *cooperate as fully and freely with the League of Nations as is possible for a non-member nation.* Cooperation with the League even in an official capacity is already an accepted part of the foreign policy of the United States. We are merely suggesting that this practice be extended to the utmost limits. The extent to which our Government has already entered into official relations with the League is not generally recognized throughout the country. The United States Government has been officially represented at the following conferences conducted by the League: Conference on Obscene Publications, Consultation on Opium Traffic, Conference on Customs Formalities, Conference on Transit and Communications, Consultation on a new Arms Traffic Convention; and has participated in the work of the Health Committee, the Advisory Committee on Anthrax, the Advisory Committee on Traffic in Women and Children. The United States is an official member of the International Hydrographic Bureau. Numerous American citizens are members of League committees and commissions, and several Americans are permanent members of the League Secretariat. Professor Manley O. Hudson recently listed the names of 123 Americans who have served the League officially in one capacity or another.[1]

---

[1] American Cooperation with the League of Nations, published by World Peace Foundation, 40 Mt. Vernon St., Boston.

As encouraging as is this evidence, it is obvious that only a beginning has been made. There are many additional ways in which the United States can participate in the activities of the League without becoming a member. The League of Nations Non-Partisan Association presented a memorial to the Secretary of State on May 2, 1925, in which attention was called to a number of additional ways by which the United States could cooperate with the work of the League, including the appointment of regular representatives of our Government on the following Commissions: Permanent Health Committee, Advisory Committee on Traffic in Opium and other dangerous Drugs, Advisory Committee on Traffic in Women and Children, Permanent Mandates Commission, Economic and Financial Committee, Coordination Commission on Reduction of Armaments; and by ratification of certain specified general treaties.[1]

But increased cooperation, without membership in the League, is not sufficient to meet the needs of the situation. *The ideals and aspirations of the American people with regard to world peace can never be fully realized until the United States is a full-fledged member of the League.* It can hardly be questioned that at one period the people of the United States were overwhelmingly in favor of entrance into a league or association of nations. Prominent leaders of both political parties strongly advocated such a procedure, numerous organizations representing bar, church, education, labor, commerce, finance, endorsed the idea in countless resolutions. Then came the political campaign of 1920 with its bitter personal feuds, as a result of which the real underlying issues were obscured by passion, misrepresentation and downright falsehood. Nevertheless, so favorable was public sentiment toward entrance that the Senate would have ratified the treaty and the United

---

[1] A copy of this Memorial may be secured from the League of Nations Non-Partisan Association, 6 East 39th St., New York City.

States would have entered the League except for the refusal of President Wilson to accept the Senate reservations. There is no room for doubt that the serious illness of President Wilson, in addition to making him irritable and obstinate, prevented him from keeping in intimate touch with the situation in the Senate. It is well to remember that, in spite of the unparalleled bitterness which prevailed, the final vote on ratification with reservations attached was 49 yeas and 35 nays, that is to say, a considerable majority of senators were in favor of entrance into the League.[1] If the President had been willing to accept reservations, the required two-thirds vote could probably have been secured and we would have entered the League immediately. The reservations would have made very little, if any, difference in the effectiveness of our cooperation.

The attempt to assess responsibility for our failure to enter the League is a fruitless performance. The real question now before the people of the United States is this: Shall we continue to be blinded and paralyzed by passion and partisanship, or shall we forget the feuds of the past and determine our attitude toward the League in the light of the actual facts of the existing world situation? If all memory of the violent controversy of 1920 could be erased, can there be any doubt that the United States would enter the League without delay? We would enter the League not because we believe it to be a perfect instrument—on the contrary, its weaknesses and grave imperfections are fully recognized—but because the place for a powerful nation like the United States is on the inside, where it may aid in determining the character of its activities and the scope of its jurisdiction, rather than on the outside, indulging in harshest criticism.

Mr. Elihu Root recently said: "The important thing

[1]For an excellent review of the Senate vote on various reservations, see The United States Senate and the Treaty, published by the World Peace Foundation, 40 Mount Vernon St., Boston.

is to get the right kind of an institution started, even though it be in the most rudimentary form. There is one unfailing characteristic of human nature which comes into play when an institution is once started. It is that after an institution is established and is conspicuous and universally known, it enters into the basis of thought of the people who have to do with the subjects to which it relates. People begin to think differently about such subjects. They begin to think that way, and if the institution is so conducted as to command confidence within its original limited scope, it grows naturally and inevitably because the fundamental idea being no longer a novelty and being accepted, enlargements and improvements of the idea are soon readily accepted."[1]

If the United States is ever to enter the League, reservations to the Covenant will doubtless be necessary. Peace advocates should, therefore, be devoting serious study to appropriate reservations. In the plan which he submitted in the Bok peace contest, Professor Manley O. Hudson, of Harvard University, and a member of the Legal Section of the Secretariat of the League of Nations, suggested the following conditions of entrance into the League by the United States:

"a. Treaty of Versailles. That the United States assumes no obligation under any part of the Treaty of Versailles (or other treaty of peace) except those parts setting forth the Covenant of the League of Nations and the charter of the International Labor Organization.

"b. Constitutional limitations. That all action by the United States as a member of the league shall be subject to the limitations established by the Constitution with reference to the federal system of government and with reference to the exercise of the power to make treaties, the power to declare war, the power to make appropriations, and the power to appoint diplomatic representatives.

---

[1] Foreign Affairs, April, 1925, p. 356.

"c. Articles 10 and 16. That the United States assumes no obligation to participate in any war, or to take any action to preserve as against external aggression the territorial integrity or political independence of any member of the League under Article 10, or to adopt any economic measures of a coercive nature under article 16, except as the Congress of the United States may decide upon at the time.

"d. Domestic matters. That the United States shall remain free to determine for itself what are the matters which by international law are solely within the domestic jurisdiction of the United States, and therefore outside the competence of the Council or Assembly under Articles 11–15.

"e. Monroe Doctrine. That membership in the League shall involve no limitation on the power of the United States to pursue the policy known as the Monroe Doctrine, as it may be defined by the United States.

"f. Equality of voting. That in any dispute before the Council or Assembly, to which the United States is a party, and to which there is another party associated with a Member of the League as dominion, colony, or member of the same federation or commonwealth, such Member of the League shall also be deemed a party to the dispute for the purpose of applying Article 15.

"g. Withdrawal. That the United States may at any time withdraw from membership on its own determination that its obligations have been fulfilled."[1]

But, someone asks, would not entrance into the League involve us in the war system? The answer is that we are involved already. Let us be under no delusions at this point. Staying out of the League does not remove the risk of our becoming involved in another European war. Moreover, going into the League would not in any way increase the danger of our becoming involved in war.

[1]Ways to Peace, pp. 290, 291.

The League does not have either the power or the inclination to commit us to war. All important decisions of the Council require a unanimous vote, and with a permanent vote in the Council we could block any effort of the League to commit the nations to war.

It is true that at the present time the League may as a last resort call for the use of armed force against a recalcitrant nation, if unity of opinion can be secured in the Council. This provision must be changed if the League is to make its maximum contribution to the cause of peace. As a matter of fact, there is very slight possibility that the United States will enter the League until the articles of the Covenant authorizing the use of armed sanctions are removed. On the other hand, if the United States should offer to enter the League on condition that these provisions be eliminated, is it not wholly probable that the nations of the world would eagerly make the required changes in the Covenant?

It is sometimes said that the United States should not enter the League because the Covenant provides that the present status quo in boundaries shall not be changed by violence, thus perpetuating grave injustice in several cases. In this connection attention should be called to the fact that there are only two ways of changing boundaries or other unjust features of existing treaties: by compulsion or by agreement. Have we any assurance that the use of violence as a means of changing boundaries would result in greater justice? So far as Europe is concerned, it is almost certain that any attempt to change existing boundaries by force would result in war, perhaps in a general conflict involving many nations. The peoples who are now the victims of injustice would not, in all probability, find their position improved at the end of another war. The fact of the matter is that the only effective way to change unjust treaties is by agreement, and agreement is conditioned upon the spirit manifested by the various peoples concerned. Therefore the creation of sympathetic understanding and friendly cooperation between the nations involved is essential if injustice is to be overcome without violence. It is admitted by all persons who are acquainted with the activities of the League that it is making an incalculable contribution toward progress in this direction. The League affords the best mechanism through which unjust treaties may be revised when hatred and fear have diminished sufficiently to make this possible without war.

It should never be forgotten that if the danger of war is to be removed, effective agencies of international justice, through which disputes may be settled amicably, must be created. The important question before us, therefore, is this: In what way can the United States most effectively cooperate in strengthening international organization? If three phases of international organization are required—legislation, administration and adjudication—should we continue to talk of a mythical association of nations, or should we enter the League? As a matter of fact, efforts to secure an association of nations, as a substitute for the League, have long since been abandoned. The question has been simplified to this: Shall we stay out or shall we go in with reservations? It seems to the writer that the arguments in favor of immediate entrance, on condition that armed sanctions be removed, are overwhelming and unanswerable.

The complex and dangerous problems of our modern world cannot be solved except through effective international organization. "We are suffering today," says William S. Culbertson, of the United States Tariff Commission, "from a too rapid advance in science and in commercial and industrial organization without a corresponding advance in social and governmental organization, and if the organization of the world's common life is to catch up and if we are to be secure and prosperous, the

United States must do its share to achieve and preserve world peace.'''[1]

The foreign policy of the United States in the decades just ahead may prove to be the deciding factor in determining whether or not militant nationalism, aggressive imperialism and international anarchy, are to lead to further wars, or whether an era of international peace shall be ushered in by outlawing war and by creating effective social machinery through which a new and higher conception of nationalism may find expression. For a powerful nation like the United States to continue its insistence upon absolute sovereignty and to refuse to cooperate in creating effective international agencies of justice, is to obstruct the pathway that leads away from international chaos and destruction. For if we insist upon being a law unto ourselves, we make it easier for other nations to do likewise. Surely, with so much at stake for the entire human race, the only place for the United States is in the vanguard of the movement to substitute international law for international violence, international agencies of justice for international anarchy.

CAN IT BE ACCOMPLISHED?

Is the Task of Creating Adequate International Organization Capable of Accomplishment? That we are confronted with stupendous difficulties in the effort to create adequate international organization is readily admitted by all students of world problems. There are some persons who frankly say that the task is too gigantic to be accomplished in this generation and that, therefore, the only safe policy to adopt is that of heavy military and naval preparedness. On the other hand, many serious students of international affairs believe that sufficient progress can be made in strengthening international agencies of justice within the next few decades to give us reasonable security against the

[1]Ways to Peace, p. 103.

recurrence of war. Let us examine the foundations of this hope.

To begin with, we find encouragement in the fact that every great social reform has at one period seemed to be surrounded by almost insurmountable barriers. The task of substituting law and orderly processes of justice for anarchy and violence has at every stage been confronted with heavy obstacles. Plato and Aristotle were both convinced that democratic government could not function successfully in an area larger than a city-state. Predictions of failure have been made every time an extension of governmental jurisdiction has been suggested. In the early days of our Federal Government, sceptics concerning its usefulness were found in high places. In commenting upon the feeling which prevailed, James Bryce says: "The new Constitution was an experiment, or rather a bundle of experiments, whose working there were few data of predicting. It was a compromise, and its own authors feared for it the common fate of compromise—to satisfy neither party and leave open rents which time would widen."[1] Mr. Charles Grove Haines makes the following comment upon the prevailing attitude toward the Supreme Court: "Notwithstanding the wide constitutional authority enjoyed and a group of strong judges—the Supreme Court was slow in attaining a position of prominence in the national government. Chief Justice Jay resigned after only a few years' service and when tendered a reappointment by President Adams in 1800, wrote: 'I left the bench perfectly convinced that under a system so defective it would not obtain the energy, weight, and dignity which are essential to its affording due support to the national government, nor acquire the public confidence and respect which, as the last resort of the justice of the nation, it should possess. Hence I am induced to doubt both the propriety and expediency of my returning to the

[1]Studies in History and Jurisprudence, p. 304.

bench under the present system.' On August 5, 1792, Edmund Randolph, wrote to Washington: 'So crude is our judiciary system, so jealous are our state judges of their authority, so ambiguous is the language of the Constitution, that the most probable quarter, from which an alarming discontent may proceed, is the rivalship of these two orders of judges.' "[1]

We Americans are so familiar with the operation of democratic government over enormous areas that we fail to realize the significance of our Federal Government. In spite of much corruption and grave inefficiency at times, our system of government has on the whole operated extraordinarily well. It should be recognized, of course, that many of our people have had a common heritage of racial stock and culture, although this is not true to the extent that is sometimes supposed. The people of the United States have come from many lands. There are now more than fourteen million foreign born people in the United States. There are two million foreign born people in New York City alone; while Chicago has 805,000; Philadelphia 397,000; Detroit 289,000; Cleveland 239,000. If the children of these people be added, it is obvious that a not inconsiderable proportion of our total population is made up of first and second generation immigrants. There is no spot in the world where such vast numbers of diverse peoples are crowded together as in the City of New York, with its 479,000 Russians; 390,000 Italians; 203,000 Irish; 194,000 Germans; 145,000 Poles; 126,000 Austrians; and scores of thousands of many other nationalities. And yet the astounding fact is that these various peoples live together with very little friction. To our forefathers the present government of New York City would have been regarded as an utter impossibility. If various races and nationalities can live together peaceably in the United States, why is it not within the bounds of

[1]The Conflict over Judicial Powers in the United States to 1870, p. 45.

possibility that they can learn to live this way throughout the earth? Switzerland affords a striking example of three races—Frenchmen, Germans and Italians—living together amicably under one government, although maintaining three official languages.

The experience of the British Commonwealth also offers us great encouragement. "The British Commonwealth today," says Philip Kerr, "is a free association of independent nations—Great Britain, Canada, Australia, New Zealand, South Africa and Ireland. These six nations compose it; none can dictate to the other. The only constitutional link is the Crown, fundamentally a symbol of their unity." India also is rapidly moving toward dominion status or absolute independence. In spite of the vast numbers of people and the different races involved and the great distances separating the various parts, the British Commonwealth is functioning sufficiently well to offer hope for effective international agencies.

Moreover, the World Court, the League of Nations and the International Labor Organization have themselves made astounding progress during their brief lifetime. It should not be forgotten that they were born at a period when national fear, suspicion and hatred were at a very high peak, and that they have been confronted at every stage with stupendous obstacles, arising out of insistence upon extreme national sovereignty, the maintenance of huge armaments and the disposition to use force in the effort to secure a desired end, and aggravated by the extreme complexity and vastness of the problems requiring solution. Moreover the continued absence of the United States, Germany and Russia from membership in the League has placed an incalculably heavy burden upon its activities. The fact that the League is linked up with the Treaty of Versailles, which is regarded in many quarters as a vindictive and unjust document, has added greatly to its difficulties. When all these facts are kept in mind, the more marvelous do the actual achievements of these international agencies appear.

There is every reason to believe that even more rapid progress will be made in the near future than has been true of the past. There is much evidence to indicate that Europe is beginning to settle down, after the wild debauch of hatred and violence of the past decade. Passions are cooling off. The futility and suicidal nature of war are becoming more obvious. The spirit of international cooperation is growing rapidly. As Mr. William S. Culbertson has pointed out: "International government is not a thing to be created; it exists now and the United States is a party to it . . . The significance of this world treaty structure, which is too often taken for granted, should be emphasized, for it is an admission of the principle that national security and prosperity do depend upon cooperation with—giving to and taking from —other nations. It has produced a vast network of bilateral and multilateral treaties and international arrangements." Fortunately, also, the physical basis for international cooperation is being more firmly established each decade. Space is being bridged and time eliminated by modern inventions. Moreover, there is a rapid advance in popular education throughout the world. The common people, who everywhere abhor war, are gaining power and are certain to exercise increasing influence in international affairs. "As nearly as I can estimate," says Mr. Oscar Newfang, "not over three million square miles, or about 6 per cent, of the total land area of the earth, amounting to 57,000,000 square miles, is now under autocratic and irresponsible government; or in terms of population not over 115,000,000, or about 7 per cent of the total population of the earth, estimated at 1,700,000,000."[1] Furthermore, the process of unifying of mankind has already advanced a very considerable pace. There are only about

---

[1]The Road to World Peace, p. 131.

sixty nations in the world today, as compared with the hundreds of petty principalities in Europe alone a few centuries ago.

Many of the most acute problems of Europe are now on the road to solution. The Dawes Plan has helped to stabilize conditions in Germany and elsewhere in Europe, although there are many experts who believe it requires further modifications. The Ruhr has been evacuated, thus bringing to an end Poincare's mad policy of strangulation. Cologne and other Rhineland cities are soon to witness the departure of Allied troops. At the moment of writing it seems probable that the security pact between Germany, France, Great Britain and Belgium will be signed, and that Germany will enter the League very shortly. If these momentous events actually come to pass, there is reason to believe that it may be possible to eliminate armed sanctions entirely from the League. Especially is this probable if the United States enters the World Court without further delay, and resolutely supports all efforts to secure an international agreement outlawing war. If the right to use armed force is abandoned by the League, the most powerful argument against America's entrance will thereby be removed. If the United States Government should say to the other nations: We are willing to enter the World Court now; we desire to see an international agreement reached outlawing war as a public crime, and will cooperate with all efforts directed toward this end; we are prepared to enter the League when war is outlawed and armed sanctions are removed from the League—if we would say something like this, can there be any doubt that the response from the peoples and governments of Europe would be immediate and effective? For us to refrain from taking this action would be a fatal blunder and a terrible crime against humanity. With Germany and the United States in the League, and with Russia ultimately becoming a member, a great hope would spring up in the hearts of people everywhere, the hope that war is to be abolished by international understanding and cooperation, functioning through appropriate international agencies.

And so the answer to the question, "Is the task of creating adequate international organization capable of achievement?" depends upon what we and the other peoples of the earth do. The odds against us are heavy, the task is a stupendous one, the barriers are high and the obstacles enormous, but . . . Sufficient progess has already been made to make us hopeful that if the nations would cooperate wholeheartedly, international organization at least adequate to postpone war and give further time in which to generate the spirit and perfect the mechanism of peace could actually be created in this generation.

If this task is to be accomplished, faith and works are essential; faith in the fundamental unity of mankind, faith in law and orderly processes of justice as a better foundation for security than that afforded by armaments, faith in the moral power of public opinion and other non-violent means of securing fulfillment of international agreements; works, manifold and continuous in the field of education and politics, until peoples everywhere are aroused to the dangers of international anarchy and war, informed as to the underlying issues in international affairs, and determined to abandon and outlaw the war system and to extend the sphere of orderly government to include relationships between nations. Here is a task at once difficult and dangerous and yet capable of accomplishment. For the first time in human history, it is now within our power to adopt certain practical measures which, if adopted, will remove the probability, although not the possibility, of another great war. No more thrilling challenge confronts the people of this generation than that inherent in the crusade to abolish war and to create adequate international organization. We can do it if we will!

APPENDIX A

BIBLIOGRAPHY

1. Syllabus on International Relations, by Parker Thomas Moon. An absolutely invaluable bibliography. $2.00.
2. The Permanent Court of International Justice, by Manley O. Hudson, $4.00.
3. Introduction to the Study of International Organization, by P. B. Potter. $4.00.
4. League or War, Irving Fisher, $2.00.
5. America's Interest in World Peace, Irving Fisher, $1.00.
6. Ideals and Realities in Europe, Margaret Wrong, $.75.
7. The Rebuilding of Europe, Ruth Rouse, $.75.
8. America and World Peace, by Justice John H. Clarke, $1.50.

   Books by authors who are opposed to the entrance of the United States into the League of Nations as at present constituted:

9. Security Against War, by Frances Kellor, $6.00.
10. America's Place in the World, by Herbert Adams Gibbons, $2.00.
11. A Study of International Government, by Jessie W. Hughan, $2.75.
12. International Society, by Philip M. Brown, $1.50.

Pamphlets

13. The United States and the Permanent Court of International Justice, including the Statute of the Court and various important documents, five cents.
14. The Permanent Court of International Justice, by John Bassett Moore, five cents.
15. League of Nations Year Book, twenty-five cents.
16. An American Peace Policy, by Kirby Page, $.15 paper, $.75 per dozen, $6.00 per hundred, cloth $1.00.
17. Imperialism and Nationalism, by Kirby Page, paper $.15, cloth $1.00.
18. War, Its Causes, Consequences and Cure, Kirby Page, paper $.15, cloth $1.50.
19. The Abolition of War, Sherwood Eddy and Kirby Page, paper $.15, cloth $1.50.
20. Christian Fellowship among the Nations, Davis, Chamberlain, $.25.

21. Protocol for the Pacific Settlement of International Disputes, five cents.
22. A Practical Plan for Disarmament (the so-called Shotwell-Bliss-Miller Plan) five cents.
23. Plans and Protocols to End War, by James T. Shotwell, five cents.
24. America's Part in Advancing the Administration of International Justice, Edwin B. Parker, five cents.
25. Facts: Studies in International Relations (in chart form) $.25.
26. Chart of the League of Nations and the Permanent Court of International Justice, five cents.
27. The Harding-Coolidge World Court Measure, by Frederick J. Libby, five cents.
28. The Work of the Permanent Court of International Justice, by Manley O. Hudson.

Any of these publications may be secured from

KIRBY PAGE

347 Madison Avenue   New York City

APPENDIX B

The following societies will be glad to provide further information in regard to different phases of the World Court issue and to make suggestions in regard to speakers and literature:
World Peace Foundation, 40 Mt. Vernon St., Boston, Mass.
The League of Nations Non-Partisan Association, 6 East 39th Street, New York, N. Y.
The American Association for International Conciliation, 405 West 117th Street, New York, N. Y.
The American Peace Award, 565 Fifth Ave., New York, N. Y.
American Committee for the Outlawry of War, 134 So. La Salle Street, Chicago, Illinois.
National Council for Prevention of War, 532 Seventeenth Street, Washington, D. C.
Federal Council of Churches, 105 E. 22nd Street, New York, N.Y.
World Alliance for Friendship through the Churches, 70 Fifth Avenue, New York, N. Y.
Fellowship of Reconciliation, 383 Bible House, New York, N.Y.
Fellowship of Youth for Peace, 104 East 9th Street, New York, N. Y.
Council of Christian Associations, 600 Lexington Ave., New York, N. Y. or 347 Madison Ave., New York, N. Y.

APPENDIX C

DATA CONCERNING THE PERMANENT COURT OF
INTERNATIONAL JUSTICE[1]

ORIGIN. The Permanent Court of International Justice realizes a policy which has been advocated by the United States Government for more than 50 years. The American delegations to the Hague Conferences in 1899 and 1907 supported the formation of a court, which, however, failed to come into being. Art. 14 of the Covenant of the League of Nations provides for the establishment of such a court. In fulfillment of this provision the Council of the League on February 13, 1920, appointed an Advisory Committee of Jurists to formulate the scheme of its organization.

The draft statute of the Advisory Committee of Jurists was examined by the Council of the League at its meeting July 30–August 4, and the Council decided to communicate the draft scheme for the institution of the Court to the Governments Members of the League. It was studied by the Council at Paris on September 16 and finally approved by it at Brussels on October 20–28.

The draft statute was submitted to the First Assembly of the League at Geneva in November, 1920. The Assembly by a unanimous vote on December 13, 1920, approved the resolution providing that the Statute be appended to a protocol which should be submitted within the shortest possible time to the Members of the League of Nations for ratification. Ratifications were promptly made, and the Second Assembly and Council of the League of Nations on September 14–15, 1921, proceeded to the election of the 11 Judges and the four Deputy Judges of the Court.

STATES ACCEPTING THE COURT PROTOCOL—48

Albania	Dominican Republic	Norway
Australia	Esthonia	Panama
Austria	Finland	Paraguay
Belgium	France	Persia
Bolivia	Greece	Poland
Brazil	Haiti	Portugal
British Empire	Hungary	Rumania
Bulgaria	India	Salvador
Canada	Italy	Serb-Croat-Slovene State
Chile	Japan	Siam
China	Latvia	South Africa, Union of
Colombia	Liberia	Spain
Costa Rica	Lithuania	Sweden
Cuba	Luxemburg	Switzerland
Czechoslovakia	Netherlands	Uruguay
Denmark	New Zealand	Venezuela

[1]This appendix is taken from the Yearbook of the League of Nations, 1925.

MEMBERS ACCEPTING COMPULSORY JURISDICTION—23

Austria	Finland	Norway
Brazil	France[1]	Panama
Bulgaria	Haiti	Portugal
China	Latvia	Salvador
Costa Rica	Liberia	Sweden
Denmark	Lithuania	Switzerland
Dominican Republic	Luxemburg	Uruguay
Esthonia	Netherlands	

JUDGES OF THE COURT

Elected Septmeber 14-15, 1921, to serve nine years

Judge	National of	Born
Hans Max HUBER, President	Switzerland	1874
Rafael ALTAMIRA y Crevea	Spain	1866
Charles André WEISS, Vice-President	France	1858
Dionisio ANZILOTTI	Italy	1869
Antonio Sanchez de BUSTAMANTE	Cuba	1865
Robert Bannatyne Viscount FINLAY	Great Britain	1842
Bernard Cornelis Johannes LODER	Netherlands	1849
John Bassett MOORE	United States	1860
Didrik Galtrup Gjedde NYHOLM	Denmark	1858
Yorozu ODA	Japan	1868
Epitacio da Silva PESSÕA[2]	Brazil	1865

DEPUTY JUDGES

Frederik Valdemar Nikolai BEICHMANN	Norway	1859
Mikhailo JOVANOVICH	Serb-Croat-Slovene State	1853
Demitrie NEGULESCU	Rumania	1876
WANG Ch'ung-hui	China	1882

JUDGMENTS[3]

No.	Parties	Subject	Date rendered
1	Great Britain, France, Italy and Japan; Poland, intervener—Germany	S. S. Wimbledon; freedom of Kiel Canal	August 17, 1923
2	Greece—Great Britain	Mavrommatis Palestine Concessions	August 30, 1924
3	Bulgaria, Greece (summary procedure)	Treaty of Neuilly, Art. 179, Annex, par. 4 (interpretation)	September 12, 1924
4	Bulgaria, Greece (summary procedure)	Interpretation of Judgment No. 3	March 26, 1925
5	Greece—Great Britain	Mavrommatis Jerusalem concessions	March 26, 1925
6	Germany—Poland	German interests in Polish Upper Silesia	

[1]Contingent on entrance into force of the protocol for the pacific settlement of international disputes.

[2]Elected September 10, 1923, to succeed Ruy Barbosa (d. March 1, 1923).

[3]All documentary publications of the Permanent Court on sale and obtainable from World Peace Foundation, American agent, 40 Mt. Vernon St., Boston, Mass.

ADVISORY OPINIONS

Given at the request of the Council of the League of Nations

No.	Cases or Statements by	Subject	Date rendered
1	Great Britain, Netherlands, International Federation of Trades Unions, International Federation of Christian Trades Unions, International Labor Office	Nomination of delegates to the International Labor Conference	July 31, 1922
2	Great Britain, France, Hungary, Portugal, International Agricultural Commission, International Labor Office, International Federation of Trades Unions	Agricultural labor and the International Labor Organization	August 12, 1922
3	Great Britain, France, Hungary, Portugal, International Agricultural Commission, International Labor Office, International Federation of Trades Unions	Agricultural production and the International Labor Organization	August 12, 1922
4	France and Great Britain	Nature of dispute about nationality decrees in Tunis and Morocco (French zone)	February 7, 1923
5	Finland	Dispute over the autonomy of Eastern Carelia	July 23, 1923
6	Germany and Poland	Protection of German settlers in Poland	September 10, 1923
7	Germany and Poland	Acquisition of Polish nationality by German settlers	September 15, 1923
8	Czechoslovakia and Poland	Jaworzina boundary	December 6, 1923
9	Albania, Greece and Serb - Croat - Slovene State	Saint Naoum Monastery (Albanian frontier)	September 4 1924
10	Greece and Turkey	Exchange of Greek and Turkish populations	February 21, 1925
11	Poland and the Free City of Danzig	Polish postal boxes in Danzig	May 16, 1925

PROPOSAL FOR ACTION BY UNITED STATES

The President of the United States on February 24, 1923, transmitted to the Senate a message in which he sought the advice and consent of that body to ratification of the protocol and Statute under special conditions.

A resolution embodying conditions of acceptance by the United States is to be considered by the Senate beginning December 17, 1925, as follows:

TEXT OF SENATE RESOLUTION 5
(With the Harding-Hughes-Coolidge Reservations)

Whereas the President, under date of February 24, 1923, transmitted a message to the Senate accompanied by a letter from the Secretary of State, dated February 17, 1923, asking the favorable advice and consent of the Senate to the adhesion on the part of the United States to the protocol of December 16, 1920, of signature of the statute for the Permanent Court of International Justice, set out in the said message of the President (without accepting or agreeing to the optional clause for compulsory jurisdiction contained therein), upon the conditions and understandings hereafter stated, to be made a part of the instrument of adhesion: Therefore be it

Resolved (two-thirds of the Senators present concurring), That the Senate advise and consent to the adhesion on the part of the United States to the said protocol of December 16, 1920, and the adjoined statute for the Permanent Court of International Justice (without accepting or agreeing to the optional clause for compulsory jurisdiction contained in said statute), and that the signature of the United States be affixed to the said protocol subject to the following reservations and understandings, which are hereby made a part and condition of this resolution, namely:

1. That such adhesion shall not be taken to involve any legal relation on the part of the United States to the League of Nations or the assumption of any obligations by the United States under the covenant of the League of Nations constituting part 1 of the treaty of Versailles.

2. That the United States shall be permitted to participate through representatives designated for the purpose and upon an equality with the other States, members, respectively, of the council and assembly of the League of Nations, in any and all proceedings of either the council or the assembly for the election of judges or deputy judges of the Permanent Court of International Justice or for the filling of vacancies.

3. That the United States will pay a fair share of the expenses of the court as determined and appropriated from time to time by the Congress of the United States.

4. That the statute for the Permanent Court of International Justice adjoined to the protocol shall not be amended without the consent of the United States.

5. That the United States shall be in no manner bound by an advisory opinion of the Permanent Court of International Justice not rendered pursuant to a request in which it, the United States, shall expressly join in accordance with the statute for the said court adjoined to the protocol of signature of the same to which the United States shall become signatory.

The signature of the United States to the said protocol shall not be affixed until the powers signatory to such protocol shall have indicated, through an exchange of notes, their acceptance of the foregoing reservations and understandings as a part and a condition of adhesion by the United States to the said protocol.

INDEX

A

Abbott, Lyman, 23.
Abolition of War, 65, 66.
Abolition of War, The, Kirby Page, 66.
Adjudication, 18, 77.
Administration, 18, 77.
Allen, Florence E., 63.
Alliances, Military, 16.
American Cooperation with the League of Nations, World Peace Foundation, 71.
American Journal of International Law, 24.
American Supreme Court as an International Tribunal, Herbert A. Smith, 26.
Annals of the American Academy, 24, 55.
Armaments, 16, 54.
Austria-Hungary, 16.

B

Balance of Power, The, 16.
Belgium, 56, 69, 83.
Bibliography, 85.
Bliven, Bruce, 63.
Blockade, Economic, 31.
Borah, Senator, 40, 43.
Boycott, Economic, 31.
Borchard, Edwin, 50.
Brent, Charles H., 63.
British Commonwealth, 81.
Brown, Philip M., 37.
Brutum Fulmen, James N. Rosenberg, 25.
Bryce, James, 79.

C

Cadman, Sir John, 12.
Carnegie Endowment for International Peace, 67.

Carter, E. C., 63.
Cause and Cure of War, J. W. Garner, 40.
Chamberlain, Austen, 15.
Civil War, The, 27.
Clarke, John H., 63.
Codification of American International Law, James Brown Scott, 42.
Columbia Law Review, 25.
Conflict Over Judicial Powers in the United States, Letter of Edmund Randolph, 80.
Congressional Government, Woodrow Wilson, 53.
Constitution, United States, 22.
Constitutional Convention, 25, 51.
Continental Congress, 50.
Coolidge, Calvin, 29, 57, 59.
Cowling, Donald J., 63.
Croly, Herbert, 63.
Culbertson, Wm. S., 16, 77, 82.
Current History, 13.

D

Dawes Plan, The, 83.
Dawn of World Peace, The, President Taft, 9.
Debates in the Federal Convention of 1787, Edited by J. B. Scott and G. Hunt, 26, 51.
Debates in the Several State Conventions, etc., Edited by Jonathan Elliott, 51.
Debates on the Adoption of the Federal Constitution, Jonathan Elliott, 26.
Debts, European War, 13.
Democracy, 79.
Dial, The, 9.
Disarmament, 32.
Disputes, International, 43, 65.
Dreier, Mary, 63.